W9-BNE-607

300
ORCHIDS

300
ORCHIDS
Jane Boosey

Species, Hybrids & Varieties
in Cultivation

FIREFLY BOOKS

A FIREFLY BOOK

With contributions by:
Amy-Jane Beer, **David Morgan**, and **Henry Oakeley**

Published by Firefly Books Ltd. 2007

Copyright © 2007
The Brown Reference Group plc

All rights reserved. No part of this publication may be
reproduced, stored in a retrieval system, or transmitted in any
form or by any means, electronic, mechanical, photocopying,
recording or otherwise, without the prior written permission of
the Publisher.

First printing

Publisher Cataloging-in-Publication Data (U.S.)

Boosey, Jane, 1955-
       300 orchids : species and varieties in cultivation / Jane
Boosey
[528] p. : col. photos. ;   cm.
Includes bibliographical references and index.
Summary: Introduction to orchids, with description and
illustrations of 300 species, worldwide.
ISBN-13: 978-1-55407-296-5
ISBN-10: 1-55407-296-4
1. Orchids. I. Three hundred orchids. II. Title.
635.9344 dc22   SB409.B667 2007

Library and Archives Canada Cataloguing in Publication

Boosey, Jane
       300 orchids : species and varieties in cultivation / Jane
Boosey.
Includes bibliographical references and index.
ISBN-13: 978-1-55407-296-5
ISBN-10: 1-55407-296-4
       1. Orchids. 2. Orchids–Pictorial works. 3. Orchid culture.
I. Title. II. Title: Three hundred orchids.
SB409.B72 2007   635.9'344   C2007-900843-7

Published in the United States by
Firefly Books (U.S.) Inc.
P.O. Box 1338, Ellicott Station
Buffalo, New York 14205

Published in Canada by
Firefly Books Ltd.
66 Leek Crescent
Richmond Hill, Ontario L4B 1H1

The Brown Reference Group plc:
(incorporating Andromeda Oxford Limited)
8 Chapel Place, Rivington Street,
London EC2A 3DQ

www.brownreference.com

For the Brown Reference Group plc:
Editorial Director: Lindsey Lowe
Project Editor: Graham Bateman
Editor: Virginia Carter
Design: Martin Anderson, Steve McCurdy

Page 1 *Angraecum compactum*, Eric Hunt

Page 2-3 x *Burrageara* 'Nelly Isler', Photos Horticultural

Cover Photos
Front Cover: *Phalaenopsis* hybrid (Dou-dii Rose x Ching Her
              John), Global Book Publishing Library/James Young
Spine: *Oncidium variegatum*, Shutterstock/Stuart Elflett
Back cover: *Phalaenopsis aphrodite* 'Plantation',
              Shutterstock/Anne Kitzman

Printed in China

Contents

CONTENTS

Introduction

The plants covered in *300 Orchids* are part of the largest family (Orchidaceae) of flowering plants, with up to 20,000 species and about 800 genera, and the number continues to grow as new discoveries are made. They occur in numerous forms from epiphytes in the understory and canopy of tropical forests or in deciduous forests and in scrubland, to terrestrial plants growing in grassy and marshy areas of temperate regions, and to lithophytes on rocky outcrops, on rocks by rivers or on shale slopes on mountainsides. This amazing family is still evolving and diversifying in response to different conditions, especially in the tropics. Orchids quite often perform a vital role in natural ecosystems and have complex interactions with insects and other animals, which act as pollinators. In some cases they are also a source of food and shelter for insects.

Orchids are prized for their spectacular flowers, and the number of wild species is far exceeded by the number of artificial hybrids bred as part of the booming orchid industry for the cut-flower and pot-plant trade. Yet many orchids are now endangered as a result of habitat loss and over collecting (often illegally) from the wild. Many species are adapted very precisely to their specific environment and unfortunately this can work against them when that environment changes. Adaptation takes time, and in certain situations—for example, in the case of deforestation—time is the one thing they do not have.

Seed-raised plants have been used in conservation programs, such as reintroductions. Each seedling brings with it its own unique gene compliment, and greater genetic diversity in a population allows more flexibility, enabling a species to adapt to changing environmental conditions. On the positive side many local and international laws for controlling and regulating the trade have been introduced, and keen orchid keepers play an important role in maintaining stocks of endangered species.

ABOUT THIS BOOK

300 Orchids presents a cross section of species and hybrids frequently available to the general public through the orchid trade, as well as some more unusual species cultivated by orchid enthusiasts. Within the book there are a number of types of description:

Genus Entries. These are divided into three elements: *Data*, *Main Article*, and *Photograph*.
Data
- *Number of Species* indicates the number of species in the genus.
- *Classification* gives the full botanical name, the orchid hunter's name, and the year it was first discovered and described.
- *Form* describes the key characteristics of the genus.
- *Distribution* indicates where the species can be found in the wild.
- *Habitat* outlines the type of habitat in which it is found in the wild.

Main Article presents additional background information about the genus, including general cultivation methods for members of that genus.
Photograph depicts a member of the genus.

Species Entries. These follow on from many of the genus entries and describe the key characteristics, cultivation methods, and classification of representative species, together with an illustration of each species.

Picture Galleries. These galleries illustrate other species and hybrids within a genus, giving a wider representation of the huge variety of orchids.

ORCHID FORM AND STRUCTURE

Although it is the largest flowering plant family, the group as a whole shows less vegetative and floral diversity than many smaller families. There are, however, several characteristics that distinguish orchids. Their seeds are minute and dustlike and are produced inside, in a capsule. The seeds may take up to 18 months to germinate and a further 18 months to

Above: Terrestrial orchid Dactylorhiza maculata.

Right: Parts of Paphiopedilum concolor, *a terrestrial orchid.*

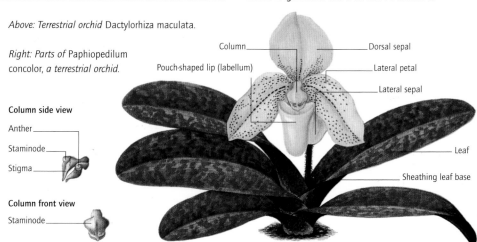

Column

Pouch-shaped lip (labellum)

Dorsal sepal

Lateral petal

Lateral sepal

Leaf

Sheathing leaf base

Column side view

Anther

Staminode

Stigma

Column front view

Staminode

mature into flowering plants. Unlike other seeds, they have no endosperm (part of the seed where food is stored) and therefore depend on an external food source for nutrients throughout germination. For successful growth in the wild orchid plants almost always maintain a symbiotic relationship with various species of fungi. This is a relationship of mutual benefit to the two species concerned—the fungi providing nutrients during germination and until the orchid is established, and the fungi benefiting from sugars from the orchid when it is able to photosynthesize.

Leaves and Stems. The leaves of orchids are quite unremarkable. They are simple in shape, often fleshy and sheathing around the base of the stem, and frequently arranged in two rows. In some species leaves are reduced to scales. Many tropical and subtropical orchids, both terrestrial and epiphytic, possess special water and nutrient storage organs called pseudobulbs, from which leaves arise. Pseudobulbs vary from hardly swollen stems to applelike organs, and may be solitary or clustered. In some species the pseudobulbs may be spaced out along a creeping or climbing rhizome.

Pseudobulbs are always on or above the soil, although some terrestrial temperate orchids have swollen roots (tubers) below soil level. It is the testiculate resemblance of these tubers that led the Greeks to call them *orchis*, their word for "testicles," and from which the term "orchid" is derived.

Flowers. It is the structure of flowers that distinguishes orchids from all other plants. They mostly contain both male and female reproductive organs and are borne alone or grouped in inflorescences, typically

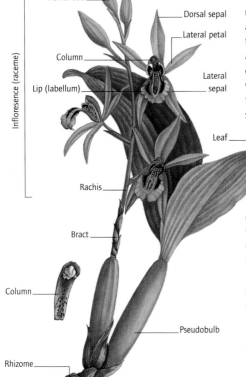

Inflorescence (raceme)

Flower bud

Dorsal sepal

Lateral petal

Column

Lateral sepal

Lip (labellum)

Leaf

Rachis

Bract

Column

Pseudobulb

Rhizome

Left: Parts of Coelogyne parishii, *an epiphytic orchid.*

racemes, spikes, or panicles. Characteristically they have three sepals and three petals. The sepals are usually similar, but the two laterals or the single dorsal may be elongated or bear a crest. The petals are usually dissimilar, with the two laterals being distinct from the dorsal, which is termed the lip (or labellum) and gives the orchid flower its characteristic appearance.

The two lateral petals and the sepals are often very similar, in which case they are known as tepals. The lip may be divided into lobes and is most often larger than the other petals. Its surface can be ornamented with plates, hairs, calluses, or keels, and often has bizarre color combinations distinct from the rest of the flower. The lip may be extended backward as a spur.

The sexual organs in orchids are united into a single structure called the column. In its simplest form, the anthers are at the top with the stigmatic surface below, the two separated by a flap known as the rostellum. There are one or two stamens with two-chambered anthers and three stigmas (one of which may be sterile, forming the rostellum). There are many variations on this basic column form. The pollen is aggregated into as many as eight waxy, horny, or mealy masses called pollinia.

At its simplest, pollination is achieved when the pollinia accidentally attach to the head or body of a bee and are then deposited on the stigma of another flower. Wasps, flies, ants, beetles, moths, hummingbirds, bats, and frogs have all been known to act as pollinators in this way. At its most specialized, pollination can involve a one-to-one relationship between a species of orchid and a species of bee. In such cases the orchid flower so closely resembles a female bee that male bees try to mate with it, a process known as pseudocopulation.

NAMING ORCHIDS

The orchid family is divided into five subfamilies, which are further divided into tribes, subtribes, and alliances. As an example, the classification of the *Cattleya* alliance is given in the accompanying table.

The scientific allocation of plant names is in a continual state of flux, and DNA studies have introduced a new facet to the assessment of relationships between species and their grouping into genera, tribes, and so on. The scientific names of the species contained in this book are generally those currently accepted in the World Checklist of "Monocots," Royal Botanic Gardens, Kew (see page 521 for the Web link).

Hybrids. In the wild it is unusual, but not totally unknown, for species

---

Classification of the *Cattleya* Alliance

Family: Orchidaceae
Subfamily: Epidendroideae
Tribe: Epidendreae
Subtribe: Laeliinae
Alliance: *Cattleya*
Genera:
  Brassavola
  Boughtonia
  Cattleya
  Encyclia
  Sulpitia
  Laelia
  Rhyncholaelia
  Schomburgkia
  Sophronitis

to interbreed and produce hybrids.
In the hands of cultivators, however,
the hybridization of orchids has reached
amazing proportions. Thousands of
stunning hybrids exist, and breeders are
constantly striving to produce new ones.
A profusion of artificially made crosses,
and even crosses of crosses, are launched
into the orchid world every year.

Many hybrids have been produced
by interbreeding species from different
genera—they are known as intergeneric
hybrids. In such cases a new and
"artificial" genus name is created. For
example, crosses between *Laelia* and
Cattleya are known as *Laeliocattleya*. To
help distinguish a "natural" genus from
an "artificial" one, a multiplication name
is often included in front, for example,
x *Laeliocattleya*. Some intergeneric
hybrids have involved up to five different
genera. As with natural genera, there are
also standard abbreviations that are used
for these hybrids, such as Lc. for x *Laeliocattleya*. In
Further References you will find Web links to detailed
listings of genera, hybrids, and their abbreviations, and
some examples are also given in this book.

Hybrid cultivars are themselves given names, most
often by the breeders. The name may reflect the
orchid's color or form, or it may be that of a person.
Cultivar names are normally presented in the following
way: x *Potinaria* 'Susan Fender.' Note the use of capital

Examples of Intergeneric Hybrids

Artificial/Hybrid Genus	Natural Genus Parents
x *Brassocattleya* (Bc.)	*Brassavola* x *Cattleya*
x *Brassoepidendrum* (Bepi.)	*Brassavola* x *Epidendrum*
x *Brassolaeliocattleya* (Blc.)	*Brassavola* x *Cattleya* x *Laelia*
x *Cattleytonia* (Ctna.)	*Broughtonia* x *Cattleya*
x *Epicattleya* (Epc.)	*Cattleya* x *Epidendrum*
x *Hawkinsara* (Hknsa.)	*Broughtonia* x *Cattleya* x *Laelia* x *Sophronitis*
x *Laeliocatonia* (Lctna.)	*Broughtonia* x *Cattleya* x *Laelia*
x *Laeliocattleya* (Lc.)	*Cattleya* x *Laelia*
x *Otaara* (Otr.)	*Brassavola* x *Broughtonia* x *Cattleya* x *Laelia*
x *Potinara* (Pot.)	*Brassavola* x *Cattleya* x *Laelia* x *Sophronitis*
x *Schombocattleya* (Smbc.)	*Cattleya* x *Schomburgkia*
x *Sophrocattleya* (Sc.)	*Cattleya* x *Sophronitis*
x *Sophrolaelia* (Sl.)	*Laelia* x *Sophronitis*
x *Sophrolaeliocattleya* (Slc.)	*Cattleya* x *Laelia* x *Sophronitis*

Standard abbreviations are shown in brackets.

letters and single quotes. Today the Royal Horticultural
Society, United Kingdom, registers new orchid hybrids—
see Web link in Further References.

CULTIVATION
Many orchid species are epiphytic (growing on trees
and other plants), some are lithophytic (growing on
rocks), while others are terrestrial (growing directly in
the ground). Their individual ecological niche is the

most important determining factor when it comes to how each species should be treated in cultivation. So when buying a plant, it is essential to ascertain the conditions of its natural habitat, in other words, the following questions should be resolved:

- Growth Habit—is it an epiphyte, a lithophyte, or a terrestrial orchid?
- Humidity—is it from humid rain forest or dry scrubland, etc.?
- Temperature—what are the normal temperature conditions in its natural habitat, including daytime and nighttime temperatures and seasonal variations (which can also be affected by the altitude at which the orchid is found in the wild)?
- Light—what are the normal light conditions, for example, does it come from a shaded habitat, such as a rain forest, or a mountainside in full sun?

Cleanliness. One of the most important aspects of greenhouse/orchid house conditions is cleanliness. Always collect up dead leaves and plants and remove any plant that looks unwell; be vigilant and thereby eradicate pests and diseases. Thorough cleaning once a year (or more often if possible) with a steam cleaner is extremely beneficial.

Air Circulation. Good circulation of air is essential—healthy plants need fresh air. The environment can soon become stale if air is not circulated. Ideally an orchid house should have an extractor fan, a

Right: An arrangement of potted orchids on a gravel-filled bench which aids drainage and maintains humidity.

small vent at mid-calf level (but screened against the incursion of bugs), and a window in the roof. As well as producing ideal conditions for growth, a through-flow of air will prevent dampening off and other fungal conditions. To avoid restricting the circulation of air around the plants do not overcrowd the bench.

Humidity. Relatively high humidity is needed in an orchid house. This can be produced by a mister, by tanks of water placed under benches, or by spraying the floor with water. Lower humidity is required during cooler months, especially in an unheated house or a house growing to cooler temperatures.

Temperatures. Broadly speaking, orchids can be grouped into three categories, defined by their temperature requirements (cool, intermediate, and warm). The ideal temperature ranges for these categories are shown in the table on the next page. By using compartments, a variety of orchids can be grown in the same house. It is perfectly possible to cultivate cool-growing orchids in a part of the orchid house with

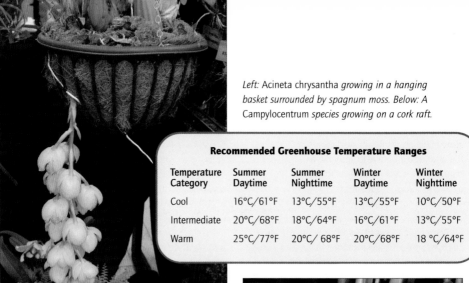

Left: Acineta chrysantha *growing in a hanging basket surrounded by spagnum moss. Below: A* Campylocentrum *species growing on a cork raft.*

Recommended Greenhouse Temperature Ranges

Temperature Category	Summer Daytime	Summer Nighttime	Winter Daytime	Winter Nighttime
Cool	16°C/61°F	13°C/55°F	13°C/55°F	10°C/50°F
Intermediate	20°C/68°F	18°C/64°F	16°C/61°F	13°C/55°F
Warm	25°C/77°F	20°C/ 68°F	20°C/68°F	18 °C/64°F

limited heating, intermediate ones where there is extra heat, and warm-growing orchids in a fully heated compartment.

Light. Most orchids prefer to be grown in dappled shade. Some, such as *Dendrobium* and *Vanda*, require stronger light in order to flower and like to be grown high up in the orchid house roof with only a thin layer of bubblewrap between them and direct sunlight. Other orchids, such as *Masdevallia* species, are happiest much lower down (even beneath the bench).

Watering. Requirements vary considerably (see details in individual genus and species accounts). In general, plants in active growth need regular watering, which should be reduced after flowering. Dormant plants simply need the medium to be kept lightly damp.

Some orchids do not like water on their leaves, whereas others, such as *Dendrobium* species, require overhead spraying with cool water to initiate flower spikes. It is always better to water early in the day. Give enough water so that it just flows out from the container.

Fertilizer. A number of fertilizer formulations are available depending on the growing medium used. Certain precautions should be taken, however. Water plants with a little plain water before applying the diluted feed, since this will avoid damage to the roots. It is often also advisable to apply the fertilizer in lower concentration and more frequently than recommended by the manufacturer. For some orchids the medium should be periodically flushed through thoroughly with water alone to prevent the build-up of salts.

Potting Medium and Containers/Mountings. Epiphytic orchids require a medium that is usually a combination of medium-sized bark, sphagnum moss, charcoal, and broken clay/terra-cotta pots. These orchids can be contained in pots, hanging baskets, or small wooden crates. Some epiphytic orchids should be mounted on pieces of tree branch (usually fruit-tree wood), bark, or cork or tree-fern slabs, in which case wrap sphagnum moss around the roots to retain moisture.

Terrestrial orchids are heavy feeders and need a planting medium consisting of peat substitute, leaf mold, and composted manure. They should be grown preferably in a raised bed either in the greenhouse or in open ground in a sheltered spot.

Recently it has become fashionable to grow *Vanda* and *Phalaenopsis* species in glass containers containing sphagnum moss and top dressed with quartz and slate chips. In this case, water infrequently with small amounts, allowing the sphagnum moss to just dry out each time; the roots must not be allowed to sit in water.

Propagation. Symbiotic germination in the presence of fungi can be carried out by extracting fungi from orchid roots and growing the fungus in Petri dishes. Orchid seeds must first be surface-sterilized with diluted bleach and then sown onto the prepared Petri dish containing the fungus. With carefully controlled temperature and light in a growth room or incubator, the seeds usually germinate in a few weeks. Alternatively, germination is possible without the symbiotic fungus as long as all the necessary nutrients are provided; this is called asymbiotic germination. The germination medium typically contains a sugar or other carbon source, minerals, vitamins, natural products, such as pineapple juice, and a gelling agent, usually agar (from seaweed).

Orchids can also be multiplied by vegetative micropropagation, in which small pieces of parent plant (explants) are used. Explants can include leaf sections,

Below: Another method of propagating orchids such as Cymbidium *species is to divide the plants using a sharp knife and repot the divisions.*

flower stems or meristem (growing tip). The explants are surface-sterilized with diluted bleach and placed onto a medium containing plant-growth regulators (the equivalent of hormones in animals), which stimulate cell growth.

PESTS AND DISEASES

Vigilance is the best defense against pests and diseases. Inspect plants thoroughly when watering and tidying; if a problem is spotted early, action can be taken to stop infestation and infection from spreading to other plants. New plants should never go into the orchid house without a period of quarantine.

Above: A home display of orchids is an attractive addition to any household. Right: Red Spider Mites can be a real pest of orchids, sucking sap from the leaves.

Bacterial Infections. Bacterial infections can result from water sitting on leaves and centers of plants or from soggy conditions in the compost. In the event of such an infection, the plant should be removed from other plants and treated in isolation. Clear away all the old compost from the roots and cut off any soft roots or damaged leaves (sterilize implements before and after use). Rinse the roots in clear water and then stand the plant for a few days in a solution made up of Neem Oil (see Glossary) and horticultural soft soap diluted in lukewarm water. If the plant looks no healthier after a few days, burn it.

Fungal Infections. A combination of very high humidity and stagnant air is ideal for fungal infections to take hold. So the first precaution is to maintain good air circulation. If black spots start to form on leaves or canes, increase the air circulation and sprinkle the plant liberally with ground cinnamon (an excellent natural antifungal agent). A drench containing Neem Oil mixed with horticultural soft soap is another good natural solution to the problem, but it must be added to the pot and not directly onto the leaves. Proprietary chemical alternatives are also available, but check they are safe for use on orchids.

Botrytis spotting appears on flowers and is often caused by a combination of high humidity and the temperature in the orchid house being a little low. Take off affected flowers and increase the temperature slightly, at the same time lowering the humidity. If these measures are not possible, take the plant indoors or to a warmer, drier atmosphere for the duration of flowering.

Viral Infections. Symptoms of virus attack include color breaks in the flowers and irregular yellow patches or black or brown rings on the leaves. Isolate any plant suspected of having a virus, have a leaf sample tested, and if a viral infection is confirmed, destroy the plant. To prevent it spreading to other plants, always sterilize cutting implements after treating each plant and control any insect pests that may transmit the virus.

Insect Pests. *Mites*. The most common mite is the microscopic Red Spider Mite. Adult females lay a single large egg that hatches into a tiny nymph, which then molts a few more times before reaching the adult stage. This entire cycle may take only a week at high temperatures. The mites feed by sucking the sap from individual cells of the leaf surface. They prefer dry conditions and often appear in heated greenhouses during the winter when their predators are less in evidence. Mite damage causes the leaves to look silvery, especially on the underside. The leaf often has many tiny yellow spots on top as well. Spider mites spin silken webs on the undersides of leaves, which show up when sprayed with a fine mist. These mites can seriously weaken plants and are also potential transmitters of disease as they move from one plant to another. To eliminate this pest, remove the affected plant from the greenhouse, water it well, and wipe away the webs. Keep it in isolation and in a slightly cooler, more humid atmosphere, repotting if necessary until there is no further evidence of infestation.

Scale Insects. Almost all species of orchids are vulnerable to attack by scale insects, which feed on plant sap, hidden beneath a hard waxy covering—the scale. Once settled on a plant, a scale insect rarely, if ever, changes position. The scale is shed several times, getting larger each time. The adult female lays her eggs underneath the shell and then dies. The eggs hatch into mobile nymphs that are easily blown around and soon find a new feeding site. Scale insects are usually found on the underside of leaves and tucked down inside dead sheaths at the base of a growth. The best method of despatching them is to use methylated spirit applied on a soft cloth or with a brush; this removes the scale on contact, and a further application will mop up any residual insects.

Aphids. Aphids suck the plant juices and, because they move easily from plant to plant, they can transmit

disease. The adult female gives birth to nymphs that start to feed and grow immediately. The nymphs molt several times and eventually mature into adult females, which are wingless if the population is small and winged if the numbers have grown. These insects are easily disposed of with a spray containing an organic or chemical insecticide.

Mealybugs. Mealybugs have a life cycle similar to that of scale insects. However, instead of having a scale they are covered with a fluffy waxy coating that protects them against many insecticides. Mealybugs tend to feed under bracts and sheaths and on roots. Under greenhouse conditions, they reproduce all year around. Mealybugs can be physically removed in the same manner as scale insects. A cotton bud or small paintbrush soaked in methylated spirit dissolves the waxy covering and is a good aid to reaching mealybugs hidden deep down in the sheaths. It is always a good idea to repot any affected orchids, using clean new compost and a fresh pot.

Slugs and Snails. Slugs and snails are notorious for damaging leaves and flower spikes. They hide in plant pots during the day and emerge to feed at night. The best way to get rid of these pests is to hand pick them off in a nocturnal offensive and put them in a container of salty solution, which will kill them instantly. Alternatively, put out small shallow dishes of beer, which they cannot resist and which results in a boozy death.

Left: Removing mealybugs using methylated spirit applied with a small paintbrush.

ORCHID HUNTERS

The Chinese word for orchid, *lan*, appears in herbals as long ago as 4,000 years. Confucius (551–479 B.C.E.) commented on the orchid's fragrance, and *Cymbidium* orchids have been cultivated by the Chinese since the Ming Dynasty which began in 1368.

Through the ages people have stolen orchids and even killed and cheated for them—once bitten by the orchid bug, it seems there is no cure. Many collectors risked life and limb hanging off rock faces in search of an elusive specimen, while others died from tropical diseases. Although such adventures are largely a thing of the past, the orchid's appeal is as strong today as it has ever been.

John Lindley (1799-1865) is said to be the "Father of Orchidology." Lindley was a professor of botany and

Above: The orchid hobby supports a large commercial industry, with growers exhibiting at shows such as the Pacific Orchid Exposition.

secretary of the Royal Horticultural Society. He wrote several books and between 1852 and 1859 he produced *Folia Orchidacea*; although never completed, it is a classic in the field of botany. Other notable figures who contributed to orchidology were Conrad Loddiges (1738-1826), Sir Joseph Banks (1743-1820), George Bentham (1800-84), Sir Joseph Paxton (1803-65)—gardener to the duke of Devonshire—Sir Joseph Dalton Hooker (1817-1911), and James Veitch (1868-1907). These are just a few names from a longer list of prominent characters, all of whom were at one time or another afflicted by "orchidomania."

Aerangis

DATA

Number of Species: About 50.

Classification: *Aerangis*
Reichenbach f. 1865; tribe
Vandeae, subtribe Aerangidinae.

Form: Leaves vary from dark
green to soft gray, growing
monopodially (upward from a
single point). Aerial roots many;
gray covered with green
chlorophyll beneath, enabling
the plant to photosynthesize
with both leaves and roots. Size
variable, some species being
substantial, others miniatures.

Distribution: Tropical Africa,
Comoros Islands, Madagascar,
and Sri Lanka.

Habitat: Various, from coastal
regions with warm growing
conditions to higher mountain
altitudes and dark tropical
forests with cooler growing
conditions. Mostly epiphytes on
trees and shrubs but occasionally
found on rocks (lithophytes)
along the banks of streams
at varying altitudes.

The name *Aerangis* is the combination of two Greek words: *aer* ("air") and *angos* ("vessel"), the latter probably referring to the spur beneath the lip which contains nectar. There are many flowers on each raceme. The flowers are often very delicate with a lacy appearance and are mostly white or cream in color. They are predominantly fragrant in the evenings, attracting moth pollinators to the nectar.

Cultivation

While members of this genus are easy to grow, it is important to know what type of habitat they come from, since those from coastal regions can cope with high light and warm evenings, while species from high altitudes or dark forests require high humidity, deep shade, and cooler conditions. Most grow well mounted on bark or cork, but some will also grow in a loose bark mix in a basket. *Aerangis* species should be watered once a week, with a fertilizer application once a month.

Found on Comoros and Madagascar, *Aerangis articulata* grows as an epiphyte on evergreen forest trees.

Aerangis citrata

A miniature shade lover from the humid coastal forests of eastern Madagascar, *Aerangis citrata* (*Angraecum citrata*) grows to just 4 inches (10 cm) in total height. Leaves are green, small, and glossy. In spring it bears long sprays of the palest yellow, waxy, lemon-scented flowers, 0.8 to 1.2 inches (2–3 cm) long.

Cultivation

Aerangis citrata is best mounted with sphagnum moss around the roots to retain moisture; the fine roots must not be allowed to dry out totally. It may also be grown in an open basket with an epiphytic compost mix. It is essential to have good air movement around the plant, which should be grown at an intermediate temperature range—during the summer, 68°F (20°C) in the daytime, dropping to 64°F (18°C) at night, and in winter, 61°F (16°C) in daytime, falling to 55°F (13°C) at night.

Classification

Aerangis citrata (Thouars) Schlechter 1914.

Aerangis citrata 'Thatched Lodge'

Aerangis luteoalba

This orchid from the Congo river basin and western Uganda is found on twigs and branches of bushes and trees, often near rivers and streams. Its tepals and column are creamy yellow. Flowers with an orange–yellow column have also been reported from western Uganda. The short-stemmed *Aerangis luteoalba* var. *rhodosticta* (*Angorchis rhodosticta*) has white or cream flowers with red columns, arranged in two flat rows. It is found in equatorial Africa, from the highlands of Ethiopia and Kenya to Mount Cameroon, and south as far as southwest Tanzania and Angola.

Cultivation

Arrange sphagnum moss around the roots, or plant in an open basket filled with epiphytic compost. Ensure the fine roots do not dry out, and maintain good air circulation and high humidity. Provide shade and intermediate temperatures of 68°F (20°C) in summer daytime, 64°F (18°C) in summer nighttime, 61°F (16°C) in winter daytime, and 55°F (13°C) in winter nighttime. Be generous with water during the summer, and apply a fertilizer once a month.

Classification

Aerangis luteoalba (Kraenzlin) Schlechter var.
A. rhodosticta (Kraenzlin) J. Stewart 1979.

Aerangis luteoalba

Aerides

DATA

Number of Species: About 25.

Classification: *Aerides* João de Loureiro, 1790; tribe Vandeae, subtribe Sarcanthinae.

Form: Leaves mid-green, growing monopodially (growing upward from a central point), very similar to those in *Vanda*. Height varies from 12 in (30 cm) to more than 5 ft (1.5 m). *Aerides* species are easily distinguished from *Vanda* by the presence of a cinnamon brown or reddish brown suffusion on the old stems and remnants of leaf bases, which is not found in *Vanda*.

Distribution: Mainly Asia: the Indian subcontinent, Nepal, Myanmar (Burma), the Philippines, Borneo, and New Guinea.

The common name of foxtail orchids describes the elongated inflorescences of these epiphytic species. The numerous fragrant flowers are waxy and pendulous, usually white, pink, or purple. The lip is frequently complex and beautiful with fringed margins and an ornate color scheme. The column has a prominent forward-projecting spur.

Aerides species are freely interfertile with species of related genera, artificially producing numerous intergeneric hybrids.

Cultivation

These orchids prefer to be grown in open baskets with a variety of loose free-draining compost, for example, large bark pieces, stone, or pieces of

Aerides leeana is found in the Philippines.

Examples of *Aerides* Hybrids

Aerides x *Arachnis* = x *Aeridachnis* (Aerdns.)

Aerides x *Asocentrum* = x *Aeridocentrum* (Aerctm.)

Aerides x *Phalaenopsis* = x *Aeridopsis* (Aerps.)

Aerides x *Trichoglottis* = x *Aeridoglottis* (Aegts.)

Aerides x *Vanda* = x *Aeridovanda* (Aerdv.)

Aerides x *Asocentrum* x *Phalaenopsis* x *Vanda* = x *Isaoara* (Isr.)

Aerides x *Renanthera* x *Vanda* = x *Nobleara* (Nlra.)

Aerides x *Renanthera* = x *Renades* (Rnds.)

Aerides x *Arachnis* x *Luisia* = x *Scottara* (Sctt.)

Abbreviations in brackets are accepted shortened forms for the hybrid.

broken pot. Growing conditions should be warm and humid (unless the species comes from a high-altitude habitat, in which case cooler conditions are required). Excellent air circulation, high light (dappled shade), generous watering, and a regular application of fertilizer (once every three to four weeks) are important.

Aerides rosea

Distributed across South China and Indochina, *Aaerides rosea* (*A. fieldingii, A.williamsii*) occurs at moderate altitudes in the East Himalayas. It is densely leafed and forms clumps growing up to 12 inches (30 cm) high. The raceme grows up to 24 inches (60 cm) and bears pendulous, closely packed flowers. These are 1 inch (2.5 cm) long, waxy, and fragrant. Flower color is usually amethyst–purple suffused with white, but very occasionally white with pale purple spots; both color variations have a whitish spur. Flowers appear in late spring to early summer.

Cultivation

Aerides rosea is best grown in an open basket with free-draining compost containing large pieces of bark, stone, and broken pots. It requires an intermediate to warm temperature range: summer daytime 68 to 77°F (20–25°C), summer nighttime 64–68°F (18–20°C), and lower in winter. Ensure the plant has good air circulation, water it generously, and apply a fertilizer every three to four weeks.

Classification

Aerides rosea Loddiges ex Lindley & Paxton 1850.

Aerides rosea

Anacamptis

DATA

Number of Species: 1 (about 20 subspecies throughout the distribution area).

Classification: *Anacamptis pyramidalis* (Linnaeus) Richard, 1818; tribe Orchidaceae, subtribe Orchidinae.

Form: This terrestrial species has four to 19 linear to lanceolate mid-green leaves arranged in a rosette, with the flowers arranged in an erect pyramidal spike approximately 12 in (30 cm) long.

Distribution: Widespread throughout Great Britain, Europe, the Mediterranean, and North Africa.

Habitat: Found on well-drained or dry downs, by roadsides, on limestone or chalk deposits, or on dunes. Plants survive well in areas where the grass is cropped regularly by grazing or is harvested for hay.

The Greek word *anakampto*, from which this species derives its name, means "to bend backward." The flowers are shaped so they can only be pollinated by butterflies and moths. Flowers do not contain free nectar, but plant saps are available to visiting insects, which break apart the cells lining the inner surface of the flower spur.

The inflorescence is unmistakably pyramidal in shape, and the flowers vary in color from white through pale or dark pink to a rich magenta. The lip has two upright ridges or folds that guide the insect's slender proboscis as if through a tunnel. The pollinia are held in a pouch above the entrance to the spur and are attached to a single sticky disk, which is saddle shaped. The disk attaches itself to the insect's proboscis as it is withdrawn from the spur. The pollinium falls forward as the butterfly or moth moves to another flower or plant and is perfectly positioned to pollinate the next flower.

A key characteristic for distinguishing *Anacamptis* from *Orchis* is that there is basal fusion of the three sepals in *Anacamptis*.

Cultivation

Because it requires very specialized conditions, this species is extremely difficult to grow. Unlike many orchids, *Anacamptis* requires well-drained rich soil. Addition of fertilizers and fungicides can kill the symbiotic root fungus that is essential for the uptake of nutrients. Collection of this species from the wild is prohibited.

Anacamptis pyramidalis

Angraecum

DATA

Number of Species: About 200.

Classification: *Angraecum* Bory 1804; tribe Vandeae, subtribe Angraecinae.

Form: Members of this genus grow monopodially (upward from a single point) with strappy pale green leaves. The lateral axillary inflorescence carries one or many flowers that are most often white but sometimes yellow, green, or ocher in color. Some are fragrant; all have a long spur at the back of the labellum (lip). Plants vary from miniatures to substantial plants of more than 6 ft (1.8 m) tall.

Distribution: Tropical Africa, Comoros, Seychelles, Mascarenes, and Madagascar.

Habitat: *Angraecum* species are in the main epiphytes but are also found as lithophytes (growing on coral and volcanic rocks) from sea level up to an altitude of 6,000 ft (1,800 m).

The name *Angraecum* is from a Malay word—*angurek*—which is also used for other epiphytic orchids in the *Vanda* alliance. The French explorer Colonel Bory de Saint-Vincent used the name *Angraecum* for a plant he collected from the island of Réunion in 1804.

The flowers of these attractive plants are well known for their showy starry quality, ranging in color from white or ivory to yellow, green, or ocher.

Cultivation

Angraecum species are easy to cultivate, although the natural habitat of individual species should be known and reproduced as closely as possible. Most of the species are happy to grow in open baskets filled with large pieces of bark and stone or in pots with free-draining compost of the same mix, at intermediate to warm temperatures. In summer during the daytime the temperature should be between 68 and 77°F (20–25°C), dropping at night to between 64 and 68°F (18-20°C). Winter temperatures should be lower, unless the plant is found at higher altitudes, when cooler conditions are called for. All of the species benefit from a good circulation of air, high humidity, and high light but dappled shade. Water generously each week, more often during the summer, with an application of fertilizer every three weeks.

A native of Madagascar, *Angraecum compactum* produces large fragrant flowers and grows well in warm to intermediate conditions.

Angraecum eburneum

Originally described on Réunion Island, *Angraecum eburneum* is known to be variable and widespread throughout eastern Kenya to eastern Tanzania (including Pemba and Zanzibar). It is widespread in coastal regions and grows both as a lithophyte (on coral and rocks) or as tree epiphytes farther inland to altitudes of 1,000 feet (300 m). The subspecies *A. eburneum eburneum* is found on islands in the western Indian Ocean.

This species is a large robust erect plant, with many fleshy roots of great length. The stems are thick and between 6 inches (15 cm) and 40 inches (100 cm) long, and 0.8 inch (2 cm) to 1.2 inches (3 cm) in diameter. The leaves are succulent or leathery and yellowish green in color. The inflorescence carries eight to 20 large flowers which are green with a white lip. The flowers also have conspicuous blackish bracts.

The differences in the size of the flowers and the length of the spur in the various localities are now used to recognize four subspecies rather than separate species as in the past.

Cultivation

Angraecum eburneum can be grown in open baskets or pots with a free-draining compost mix of large pieces of bark, stones, and broken pots. Warm conditions (summer daytime temperature of 77°F, or 25°C) are required, with a good circulation of air and high humidity. Water generously once a week (more in summer) and apply fertilizer every three weeks. High light and dappled shade are necessary.

Classification

Angraecum eburneum Bory ssp. *giryamae* (Rendle) Senghas and Cribb 1979.

Angraecum eburneum

Angraecum sesquipedale

For its showy flowers with a long spur (*sesquipedale* means "one foot and a half") this orchid is widely known as the Comet Orchid. *Angraecum sesquipedale* is widespread along the east coast of Madagascar, and subspecies *augustifolium* (Bosser and Morat. Adansonia 1972) grows in southwestern Madagascar.

The species was of great interest to Charles Darwin, who hypothesized that there must exist an insect with a proboscis corresponding in length to that of the spur of this flower. Such an insect could reach the nectar at the bottom, enabling pollination to take place. Darwin was mocked when he voiced his opinion, but some 50 years after his death a hawk moth was discovered with a proboscis long enough to pollinate the Comet Orchid. It is now named *Xanthopan morganii praedicta* (*praedicta* meaning "predicted"). The flowers are predominantly fragrant at night, luring their pollinators by smell.

Cultivation

Angraecum sesquipedale can be grown in an open basket or pot with free-draining compost of mixed bark, stone, and broken pots. Warm conditions (summer daytime temperature of 77°F, or 25°C) are required, with a good circulation of air and high humidity. Water generously once a week (more in summer) and apply fertilizer every three weeks. High light and dappled shade are necessary.

Classification

Angraecum sesquipedale Thouars 1822.

Angraecum sesquipedale

Anguloa

DATA

Number of species: 9.

Classification: *Anguloa* Ruiz & Pavón 1794; tribe Maxillarieae, subtribe Lycastinae.

Form: Growth sympodial, with large tapering pseudobulbs that bear three to five large fanlike leaves up to 39 in (1 m) long. Three to five sheathing leaves surround the base of the pseudobulb but are lost as the bulb matures. The main leaves are usually shed before the commencement of flower bud production and new growth, leaving small apical spines. Roots brown, membranous, and hairy.

Distribution: Colombia, Venezuela, Ecuador, Peru, Bolivia.

Habitat: 4,000 to 7,500 ft (1,200–2,300 m), in areas with high seasonal rainfall. May be lithophytic (usually limestone) in full sun, or terrestrial in grass or shrubs or in light woodland and woodland margins. Rarely epiphytic.

There are two main groups in the genus *Anguloa*: the white-flowered group and the red and yellow group. They are known colloquially as cradle orchids (because of the shape of *Anguloa clowesii*) or tulip orchids, since the flowers of most of the yellow and red group have an upward-facing opening formed by the petals and sepals. In the white-flowered group the flower opening faces forward. Both have a single flowering season from May to July in greenhouse culture in northern regions, with one (occasionally two) flower(s) per inflorescence, and four to 18 flowers per pseudobulb. All have a medicinal fragrance during the day and are pollinated by large bees. Flowers last for about three weeks. If pollinated, the capsule matures and splits after 12 months.

There are four natural *Anguloa* hybrids but few intrageneric hybrids, the exceptions being with *Lycaste* (*Angulocaste*) and *Ida* (*Angida*). Trigeneric crosses (*Anglyda*) are still rare.

Cultivation

All grow well in intermediate temperatures (59°F/15°C minimum at night and 86°F/30°C maximum during the day in winter), with no shade in north temperate zone winters, and light shade and 50 to 70 percent humidity in summer. With good air movement from fans, higher temperatures can be tolerated. Plants should be watered and given feed frequently, never being allowed to dry out during the growing season. On maturation of the bulb and loss of the side leaves, plants should be allowed to dry out, only watering to keep the pseudobulbs from shriveling. Use large pots filled with a free-draining compost of perlite or bark and sphagnum moss.

Anguloa uniflora from Peru.

(Text and photos Henry Oakeley)

Anguloa clowesii var. *flava*

The true *Anguloa clowesii* has a white lip and is exceedingly rare. The yellow-lipped form (*A. clowesii* var. *flava*) is commonly sold simply as *A. clowesii*. It is known as the Cradle Orchid—its petals and sepals form the "cradle" and the lip rocks back and forth freely, moving the flower. The Cradle Orchid is found in Colombia and western Venezuela where it forms, on rare occasions, the natural hybrid *Anguloa* x *ruckeri* by crossing with the Venezuelan *A. hohenlohii*.

Pseudobulbs are dark green, each one bearing three leaves up to 28 inches (71 cm) long. There are up to 18 erect inflorescences, 12 inches (30 cm) long, each with one (occasionally two) flower(s) per stem. The flowers are yellow, globose, up to 3 inches (7.5 cm) long, with a narrow opening facing upward. The lip is boat shaped, three-lobed, and distally orange, while the callus is small, flat, and hairy.

Cultivation

As with all *Anguloa* species, use a free-draining compost of perlite or bark and sphagnum moss and grow the plants in large pots. Grow at intermediate temperatures (59°F/15°C minimum winter night temperature and 86°F/30°C maximum during the day). No shade is required in north temperate zone winters, but it needs light shade and 50 to 70 percent humidity in summer. With good air movement from fans, higher temperatures can be tolerated. Water and feed well during the growing season, providing as much light and air movement as possible, commensurate with keeping the leaves cool in hot weather.

On maturation of the bulb and loss of the side leaves, plants should be allowed to dry out, and water only to keep the pseudobulbs from shriveling. This appears to stimulate flower bud production.

Classification

Anguloa clowesii Lindley 1842; *Anguloa clowesii* var. *flava* A de Candolle 1847.

Anguloa clowesii var. *flava*

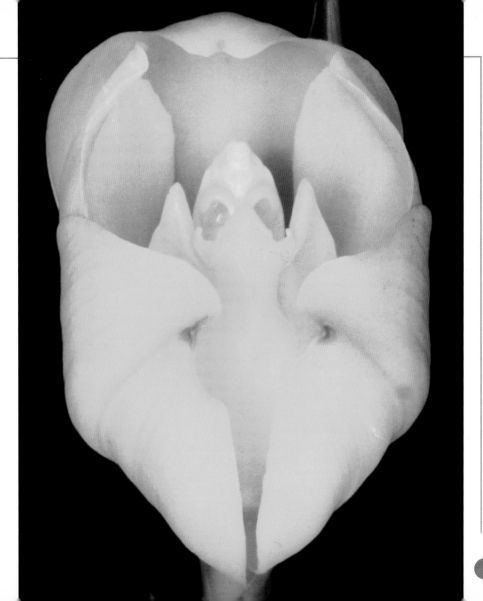

Anguloa virginalis

This is the most widely distributed of the *Anguloa* species, being found in all the countries where *Anguloa* grow. It may be found in flower in different seasons from August to May in north-central Peru, despite having only one flush of flowering. It has been misidentified as *A. uniflora* for most of the past 200 years, but is very distinct from this species. It is more easily confused with *A. tognettiae* and *Anguloa* x *speciosa* (one of its natural hybrids), but it is distinguished by the marked kink to the base of the tubular lip.

Pseudobulbs are dark green and measure 7.5 by 2.8 by 2.4 inches (19 x 7 x 6 cm). They bear three plicate leaves up to 3 feet (90 cm) long and 8 inches (20 cm) wide. Flowers appear from May to June in northern temperate zones, with up to nine erect inflorescences that grow to 18 inches (45 cm) long, and one, or rarely two, flowers.

Flowers are 3.4 inches (8.5 cm) high and 1.8 inches (4.5 cm) wide. The tips of the petals and sepals form a narrow, forward-pointing opening. The overall color is white with pink spots internally on the petals and lip and occasionally at the base of the sepals. The lip is three-lobed, tubular, and markedly kinked at the base.

Cultivation

As with all *Anguloa* species, use a free-draining compost of perlite or bark and sphagnum moss and grow the plants in large pots. Grow at intermediate temperatures (59°F/15°C minimum winter night temperature and 86°F/30°C maximum during the day). No shade is required in north temperate zone winters, but it needs light shade and 50 to 70 percent humidity in summer. With good air movement from fans, higher temperatures can be tolerated. Water and feed well during the growing season, providing as much light and air movement as possible, commensurate with keeping the leaves cool in hot weather.

On maturation of the bulb and loss of the side leaves, plants should be allowed to dry out, and water only to keep the pseudobulbs from shriveling. This appears to stimulate flower bud production.

Classification

Anguloa virginalis J. Linden ex B. S. Williams 1862.

Anguloa virginalis

Arachnis

DATA

Number of Species: About 17.

Classification: *Arachnis* Blume 1825; tribe Vandeae, subtribe Sarcanthinae.

Form: Although allied to *Vanda*, *Renanthera*, and *Dimorphorchis*, *Arachnis* is the showiest of the monopodial groups. Its members vary greatly—some have vinelike vegetation, scrambling over nearby trees and shrubs, while others grow in a more compact and close-leaved fashion. Spiderlike flowers occur on long arching sprays.

Distribution: From the Himalayas to New Guinea, the Solomon Islands, Indonesia, and Malaysia.

Habitat: *Arachnis* species are found in the wild in a wide variety of conditions, growing over rocks and boulders, or clambering up trees and over shrubs or even on the ground, often in boggy areas. They are also found at different altitudes, ranging from sea level to 4,500 ft (1,400 m).

Members of this genus are very popular orchids with enthusiasts; their showy, often fragrant flowers always fascinate and intrigue. The colors range through greens, yellows, browns, and purples, and the sepals and petals are invariably blotched by a stronger color. Their name alludes to their spiderlike appearance, and some of the species are commonly known as scorpion orchids.

Because of their fragrant and long-lived qualities, the flower sprays are much used in the cut-flower industry. As well as intrageneric hybrids, especially between *Arachnis flos-aeris* and *A. hookeriana*, many hybrids have been produced among *Arachnis*, *Vanda*, and *Renanthera* species.

Cultivation

Tall-growing, vinelike *Arachnis* can be grown successfully in specially prepared raised beds containing open free-draining compost of sphagnum moss, bark, and gritty white sand, enriched with leaf mold and manure. If the raised-bed method is not possible, then large pots containing the same type of compost will do just as well.

The smaller species prefer to be mounted on bark or slabs of tree fern with sphagnum around the roots to retain moisture. Good circulation of air is essential. They should be well watered, at least once a week for some species (more during the summer), and fertilizer should be applied regularly. Grow at intermediate to warm temperatures of 68 to 77°F (20–25°C), with high light and dappled shade. Species such as *A. annamensis* require as much sun as possible to instigate flowering.

The blotchy flowers of *Arachnis annamensis* from South Vietnam are typical of the genus.

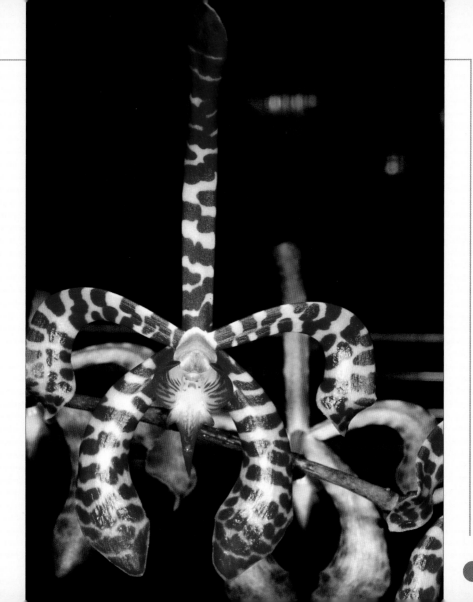

Ascocentrum

DATA

Number of Species: About 20.

Classification: *Ascocentrum*
Schlechter ex J. J. Smith 1917;
tribe Vandeae, subtribe
Sarcanthinae.

Form: The stems of this epiphytic
orchid are fleshy and densely
leaved, producing compact
plants reminiscent of *Vanda*
species, standing to about 10 in
(25 cm) tall with cordlike roots.
The flowers are borne on dense
upright racemes, each flower
with a straplike lip, a prominent
spur, and two pollinia.

Distribution: Foothills of the
Himalayas, Myanmar (Burma),
Thailand, Malaysia, the
Philippines, Java, Borneo, Taiwan.

Habitat: Humid climates, growing
on deciduous trees.

This is a small genus of monopodial epiphytic orchids allied to *Vanda* and *Ascoglossum*. The name *Ascocentrum* is from the Greek *ascos* ("bag") and *kentron* ("spur"), referring to the spur of the lip.

The inflorescences are erect conical and consist of many small flowers facing in all directions. Flower colors range from yellow to orange and rose-red to scarlet. They have a distinctive lip and back spur. While all have a compact habit, *A. pumilum* from cloud forests of Taiwan is particularly small, and some authorities place it in its own genus as *Ascolabium pumilum*.

They are widely cultivated for their showy flowers and have been widely crossed with *Vanda* species to produce many intergeneric hybrids.

Cultivation

Basket culture is best for these plants, using loose open compost that offers good drainage. Water generously once a week (more during the summer), with an application of fertilizer once every two to three weeks during the growing season. High light is needed with dappled shade. Grow in intermediate to warm temperatures and ensure a good circulation of air.

The bright orange red flowers of *Ascocentrum curvifolium* are the largest in the genus. It is found from northeast India to Indochina.

Ascocentrum ampullaceum

This compact species, sometimes called the Bird Tongue Orchid, occurs from Nepal and southwest China to Thailand. The leaves are stiff with jagged ends and have a natural spotting in mahogany that increases only when the plant is exposed to brighter light. In spring each plant is aglow with dense cerise pink flowers, about 0.5 inch (13 mm) in size, produced on racemes that form at the base of the plant between the leaf axils. The spikes are from 6 to 8 inches (15–20 cm) in size and bear 20 to 35 flowers. The flowers are long lasting and can bloom for a month or more. An orange-flowered form, *Ascocentrum ampullaceum* var. *aurantiacum*, occurs in northeast India. White forms also occur.

Ascocentrum ampullaceum has been used extensively in hybridizing, since it imparts a good flat flower and strong colors to its progeny.

Cultivation

Because this species flowers from the base of the plant, it is better suited to crate culture with loose, free-draining compost containing large pieces of bark and stone, or mounted on bark or tree fern slabs with sphagnum moss around the roots to retain moisture. Water well during the growing season and fertilize at regular intervals of two to three weeks.

High light with dappled shade is needed. Intermediate to warm temperatures (summer daytime 68 to 77°F/20 to 25°C, nighttime 64 to 68°F/18 to 20°C, lower in winter) are required, with good circulation of air.

Classification

Ascocentrum ampullaceum (Roxb.) Schlechter 1918.

Ascocentrum ampullaceum

Aspasia

DATA

Number of Species: About 9.

Classification: *Aspasia* Lindley 1833; tribe Maxillareae, subtribe Oncidiinae.

Form: Allied to several groups of the complex subtribe Oncidiinae, namely *Brassia*, *Miltonia*, *Helcia*, and *Trichopilia*. They grow epiphytically (on trees and shrubs) and are characterized by having creeping rhizomes with laterally flattened, ellipsoid, light green storage pseudobulbs. About 16 in (40 cm) in height, the pseudobulbs are short and erect and covered by leaflike bracts.

Distribution: This genus is found in the tropics of Central America from Guatemala and Nicaragua to Brazil, to an altitude of 3,000 ft (900 m).

Habitat: Often found growing on branches overhanging streams and rivers in the tropical lowland forests of Brazil.

The genus name *Aspasia* is thought to be derived from the Greek *aspasios* ("glad," or "delightful"), referring to the delightful flower; or it may be named for Aspasia, the delightful Athenian wife of Pericles in Greek mythology.

Aspasia differs from other allied genera in that the margins of the labellum (lip) are joined to the base of the column for half its length; the lamina (the broad flattened middle part of the labellum) then bends at right angles to the column. The flowers are few and are borne on an arching upright racemose inflorescence.

Cultivation

Aspasia species are easily cultivated and produce amazingly beautiful and long-lived flowers. They are ideal for the amateur grower and require abundant moisture during the growing period. Members of this genus grow well in loose medium bark in a pot or mounted. They require intermediate temperatures (68°F/20°C daytime, 64°F/18°C night, less in winter), high humidity, and good circulation of air. Water once a week (more during the summer), with an application of fertilizer once every two to three weeks during the growing season. Less water should be given during the winter, allowing for a slight drying period.

Aspasia lunata from Brazil is a spring-flowering species with flowers measuring about 1.5 inches (3.5 cm) long.

Barkeria

Number of Species: About 15.

Classification: *Barkeria* Knowles and Westcott 1838; tribe Epidendreae, subtribe Laeliinae.

Form: The genus is known for its thick roots and spindle-shaped canelike pseudobulbs, 10 to 15 in (25–38 cm) tall, enveloped by dry, transparent, thin, brown leaf sheaths. The pseudobulbs carry a few alternate long and narrow lanceolate to broadly ovate, soft-textured, deciduous leaves. Blooms vary from three to four to many, carried on a terminal racemose inflorescence.

Distribution: United States, Mexico, Costa Rica, El Salvador, Guatemala, Honduras, Panama.

Habitat: Dry scrub areas of Central America as epiphytes or as lithophytes at intermediate elevations, with *B. spectabilis* found at 5,500 to 7,000 ft (1,700–2,100 m). They grow on small shrubs and on small branches of trees, with their roots freely exposed to moving air.

The genus *Barkeria* was first described by Knowles and Westcott in 1838 and named for George Barker of Springfield, England, who had imported a plant from Mexico. *Barkeria* was once considered part of the *Epidendrum* group, but was reassigned because of structural differences in the shape of the rostellum and column, the latter having widely spreading fleshy column wings in *Barkeria*.

When not in growth, these orchids resemble a clump of dry twigs. In the spring, however, new growths are produced, which develop during the warm moist summer and eventually produce showy and long-lasting flowers in the fall and early winter. The very delicate and beautiful flowers vary from soft lilac mauve in color to cerise pink. Lateral branches sometimes develop on the inflorescence.

Cultivation

A dry bright rest period in winter is essential for this deciduous plant, which requires occasional misting but no watering. *Barkeria* species grow better mounted on wood or tree-fern slabs, with a small amount of sphagnum moss around the roots to retain moisture. Bright light is needed along with warm to cool temperatures, a good circulation of air, and high humidity. Regular applications of fertilizer (every two to three weeks) and generous watering during the warmer growing season are essential.

Barkeria lindleyana is an epiphytic species found from Mexico to Costa Rica.

Barkeria melanocaulon

This rare deciduous, epiphytic orchid is endemic to Oaxaca, Mexico, where it grows at altitudes of 330 to 1,000 feet (100–300 m). It is very delicate and beautiful, and has mauve flowers with a yellow throat and a frilly heart-shaped cerise pink lip. Carrying only four to five flowers at a time, it will flower for several months from early in the year. It is unique in the genus in having a fleshy column that diverges from the lip.

Cultivation

As with all species in the genus, it needs a dry bright rest period when it loses its leaves in winter. It is happiest mounted on bark, wood, and tree-fern slabs with moisture-retaining sphagnum moss around the roots. Water liberally during the growth season, with applications of fertilizer every two to three weeks. Warm to intermediate temperatures (summer daytime 68 to 77°F/20 to 25°C, nighttime 64 to 68°F/18 to 20°C, lower in winter), high humidity, and good air circulation are required.

Classification

Barkeria melanocaulon A. Richard and Galeotti 1845.

Barkeria melanocaulon

Barkeria spectabilis

This epiphytic species is found from Chiapas, Mexico, to Nicaragua, at 5,000 to 6,500 feet (1,500–2,000 m). Unlike other *Barkeria* species, it is normally found growing on oaks (*Quercus* species). The flowers, which appear in summer, are particularly beautiful and numerous and are washed lilac and white with purple speckling. At up to 3 inches (7.5 cm) in diameter, flowers of *Barkeria spectabilis* are the largest in the genus.

Cultivation

It needs a dry bright rest period when it loses its leaves in winter. It is happiest mounted on bark, wood, and tree-fern slabs with moisture-retaining sphagnum moss around the roots. Water liberally during the growth season, with applications of fertilizer every two to three weeks. Warm to intermediate temperatures (summer daytime 68 to 77°F/20 to 25°C, nighttime 64 to 68°F/18 to 20°C, lower in winter), high humidity, and good air circulation are required.

Classification

Barkeria spectabilis Bateman ex Lindley 1842. This species was formerly classified within *B. lindleyana*.

Barkeria spectabilis

Bifrenaria

Number of Species: About 25.

Classification: *Bifrenaria* Lindley, Gen. 1832; tribe Maxillarieae, subtribe Lycastinae/Bifrenariinae.

Form: The pseudobulbs grow in clusters and are ovoid in shape with four angles, about 2 to 3 in (5–7.5 cm) long. Each pseudobulb has one pleated leathery leaf. Inflorescences grow from base of pseudobulb, producing one to three large waxy flowers.

Distribution: Central and South tropical America (Trinidad and Tobago, French Guiana, Guyana, Suriname, Venezuela, Bolivia, Colombia, Peru, and most of Brazil).

Habitat: Growing as epiphytes or in full sun as lithophytes but mostly in rain forests at low to moderate altitudes.

Orchids in this genus are spectacular, although they are not seen very often in collections. The flowers vary in color from green to white or soft pink; they are about 2 inches (5 cm) wide and are waxy in texture. The flowers are long lasting and are sometimes fragrant.

Cultivation

Members of the genus *Bifrenaria* can be grown in pots or baskets in a mix of medium bark and stone or broken pots. They need bright light and dappled shade, with high humidity and good circulation of air. Heavy watering is essential during the period when the pseudobulbs are forming. An application of fertilizer is required every two to three weeks.

Bifrenaria tyrianthina occurs in the mountainous regions of southern Brazil.

Bifrenaria harrisoniae

Found in coastal areas of Brazil at 700 to 2,600 feet (200–800 m), *Bifrenaria harrisoniae* sometimes grows as an epiphyte on low-growing shrubs but more usually as a lithophyte on rock cliffs that are exposed to strong winds and full sun. There is very little soil material here, and the plants root deep into cracks.

The pseudobulbs are clustered and grow from 2 to 3.5 inches (5–9 cm) tall. Each pseudobulb produces a single, stiff, elliptic–oblong, pleated leathery leaf up to 12 inches (30 cm) long and 4 inches (10 cm) wide. Typically two inflorescences emerge from the base of new pseudobulbs, each bearing one or two very long-lasting and fragrant flowers. These are about 3 inches (7.5 cm) wide and have a waxy texture. Flower color varies through shades of white-washed pink with a cerise pink lip. The large three-lobed lip is hairy and purple to magenta red in color with darker veins.

Cultivation

Although this species is found growing on rocks in full sun in its natural habitat, it is best grown in bright light but with dappled shade—in full sun the leaves become damaged and yellowed. High humidity and a good circulation of air are required. Grow in pots or baskets filled with medium bark and pieces of stone or broken pots. Heavy watering is beneficial while new pseudobulbs are forming, as is an application of fertilizer every two to three weeks during the growing season.

During summer, keep daytime temperatures at between 77 and 80°F (25–27°C) and nighttime temperatures at around 66 to 68°F (19–20°C). There should be a rest period of about two months in winter when watering is stopped (apart from occasional misting). Daytime temperatures of 70 to 72°F (21–22°C) are required, with night temperatures of 58 to 60°F (14–16°C).

These plants do not like being disturbed once established, so repotting should be done only when necessary and only when new root growth has started.

Classification

Bifrenaria harrisoniae (Hooker) Reichenbach f. 1855.

Bifrenaria harrisoniae

Bletilla

Number of Species: About 5.

Classification: *Bletilla*
Reichenbach. f. 1853; tribe
Arethuseae, subtribe Bletiinae.

Form: The pseudobulbs resemble
corms and grow close to the
surface of the compost. Each
corm/pseudobulb has several
stalked and pleated leaves about
16 in (40 cm) tall.

Distribution: North Indochina to
temperate East Asia (central,
northern, and southern China,
Japan, Korea, Nansei Shoto
Myanmar, Thailand, and
Vietnam).

Habitat: This terrestrial genus
grows on grassy slopes, where
the climate is cold and dry in
the winter, and hot and very
rainy in summer.

These are almost fully hardy orchids in temperate regions and will survive all but the coldest of winters. In times of heavy frost, however, it is prudent to cover them with fleece or mulch.

The flowers in members of this genus vary from deep rose pink to white, and all species have four mealy (powdery looking) pollinia arranged in two pairs.

Species such as *Bletilla striata* are known as geophytes, since the corm has a large water storage capability that enables it to survive in the most arid conditions.

In China the corms of *Bletilla* species are used as an herbal medicine (*bai ji*). The corms are peeled and dried in the sun, before being cut into slices and ground to a powder. The powder is used with other herbs to treat lung, stomach, and skin disorders.

Cultivation

This genus can be grown in pots or in outdoor beds containing well-composted soil with good drainage. Water the plants carefully when new shoots appear, and keep them cool and dry after the leaves have fallen.

Bletilla striata is a terrestrial species from China, Japan, and Tibet.

Brassavola

Number of Species: About 20.

Classification: *Brassavola* R. Brown 1813; tribe Epidendreae, subtribe Laeliinae.

Form: This genus is characterized by its small elongated pseudobulbs with a single succulent, almost cylindrical, apical leaf; the flower stem or inflorescence grows from the apex of the pseudobulb.

Distribution: Widespread from Mexico to tropical South America.

Habitat: This genus is found in the lowlands of Central America and tropical South America growing as epiphytes; a few are found as lithophytes.

In 1698 *Brassavola nodosa* was the first tropical orchid to be taken from the Caribbean island of Curaçao to Holland; the propagation of orchids and the fascination among collectors followed soon after.

The flowers are mostly greenish and white or cream in color. They appear either singly or borne on a raceme of a few flowers. The five sepals are narrow and long. The lip is broad and fringed and partially encloses the column, which has two falciform ears. Most of the flowers in this genus produce a citruslike fragrance at night that attracts specific moth pollinators.

The genus is used widely in hybridization.

Cultivation

These orchids grow easily at intermediate temperatures (summer daytime 68 to 77°F/20–25°C, nighttime 64 to 68°F/18–20°C, lower in winter). Use an epiphytic mix of medium bark, sphagnum moss, and broken pots with perlite and charcoal added and plant in pots or baskets or mounted on bark with sphagnum moss around the roots to retain moisture. *Brassavola* species benefit from high humidity of 75 to 85 percent all year. Water freely during the active growth period and decrease watering when new growth has matured. At this time, give the plant enough water to keep the leaves from shriveling. Fertilize weekly with one-quarter- to one-half strength solution, especially while the plant is actively growing. Feed less often when the growth slows. Flush monthly with clear water to remove excess salts in the medium. Most brassavolas appreciate bright light and should be placed where they can receive plenty of light without long exposure to direct midday sun.

Brassavola tuberculata is distributed in Bolivia, Brazil, and Paraguay.

Brassia

DATA

Number of Species: About 35.

Classification: *Brassia* R. Brown 1813; tribe Cymbidieae, subtribe Oncidiinae.

Form: This genus has large elliptic pseudobulbs bearing one or two leaves at their apex. There are two papery sheaths (one on either side) emanating from the bottom of the pseudobulbs. The inflorescence emerges from the sheaths.

Distribution: Southern Florida and Mexico to tropical America.

Habitat: Most of the orchids in this genus are epiphytes but some are found as lithophytes; found in wet forests at elevations from sea level to 5,000 ft (1,500 m).

Members of this genus are commonly known as spider orchids. The slender elongated sepals and petals stretch out like spiders' legs, and the lip and two hard pollinia often resemble a spider's body. A long *Brassia* inflorescence bursting with fragrant blooms looks like rows of spiders crawling through the air. This is all part of an elaborate deception to encourage pollination. Several species in the genus are pollinated by female parasitic wasps that normally prey on particular species of spider. Normally a wasp stings a spider to paralyze it before laying eggs inside the victim to provide a meal for the developing larvae. To these wasps the markings of some *Brassia* flowers give the appearance of a spider in its web. As the wasp attempts to sting the flower, thinking it is a spider, pollination occurs.

Brassias have become more popular in recent years as orchid hobbyists and the general public have demanded more unusual and "natural" species (rather than artificial hybrids) to decorate their homes. Numerous intergeneric hybrids involving *Brassia* species are available.

Cultivation

Grow in an intermediate greenhouse (summer daytime temperatures of 68 to 77°F/20–25°C, falling to 64 to 68°F/ 18–20°C at night, lower in winter) with high humidity and good air circulation. Plants can also be grown on a suitable windowsill with a tray of damp pebbles beneath the pot. The compost should be the usual epiphytic mix of medium bark and broken pots to ensure good drainage. Generous watering is required during the growing season, and fertilizer should be applied every two to three weeks. Drier conditions are required during the winter.

Brassia arcuigera 'Punkin Patch' has a typically spidery appearance.

Brassia verrucosa

Distributed throughout Mexico to northern Brazil, *Brassia verrucosa* has thick, compressed, egg-shaped pseudobulbs. Two papery sheaths emanate from the base of the pseudobulb and two leaves, measuring up to 18 inches (45 cm) long and 2 inches (5 cm) wide, grow from the apex. The plant can often form a large clump.

The 24-inch- (60-cm-) long, horizontally arching flower spikes arise in early summer. The sepals and petals are stiffly spreading and are pale green, spotted with dark green or reddish brown. The lip is greenish white with blackish green blotches on the lower half. The flowers can be as large as 8 inches (20 cm) in diameter in the species' largest forms. The flowers are very fragrant with a heavy spicy perfume.

Cultivation

This species is easily cultivated in an intermediate greenhouse (summer daytime temperatures of 68 to 77°F/20–25°C, falling to 64 to 68°F/18–20°C at night, lower in winter) with high humidity and good air circulation. Plants can also be grown on a suitable windowsill with a tray of damp pebbles beneath the pot. The compost should be the usual epiphytic mix of medium bark and broken pots to ensure good drainage. Generous watering is required during the growing season, and fertilizer should be applied every two to three weeks. Drier conditions are required during the winter.

Classification

Brassia verrucosa Bateman ex Lindley 1840.

Brassia verrucosa

Bulbophyllum

The center of diversity and place of origin of the genus *Bulbophyllum* appears to be the mountain forests of New Guinea, where more than 600 species have been found. However, the genus is widely distributed across the tropics and occurs in Australia, Southeast Asia, (Borneo)—with over 200 species—Africa, Madagascar (more than 135 species), and tropical Central and South America.

The flowers and vegetative parts of *Bulbophyllum* species are extremely diverse; they range from root climbers, creeping their way up trees, to pendulous epiphytes or lithophytes. Some have developed almost succulent foliage and some are almost leafless, in which case their pseudobulbs are photosynthetic. Most flowers are quite small, some just a few millimetres. The foot of the column is hinged to the lip, making the lip mobile. Many flowers produce fragrances that smell of urine or rotten meat, geared to attracting fly pollinators.

Cultivation

Most species prefer to grow mounted on bark or tree-fern slabs with sphagnum moss around the roots, but they can be grown in pots or baskets with small amounts of pebbles or slate and sphagnum moss or the traditionally used medium of osmunda fiber. They are very intolerant of stale or dank compost around their roots. High humidity and a good circulation of air are essential. Generous watering is required throughout the year, with the exception of those species native to areas with a dry season (such as China, Myanmar, and the Himalayas). An application of weak fertilizer is needed once a week. Special attention should be paid to new growth—slightly less water should be given to prevent rotting.

Bulbophyllum thaiorum is distributed in Indochina.

Bulbophyllum frostii

This stunning miniature orchid from Vietnam has beautiful flowers that resemble Dutch clogs. A compact grower, it flowers freely, blooming off and on throughout the year.

Bulbophyllum frostii grows as an epiphyte on shrubs and trees. Spaced 0.5 inch (13 mm) apart on a creeping rhizome, the 0.75-inch- (19-mm-) long pseudobulbs are fat and squat with a dark green oval leaf at the top. Flowers appear in clusters from the base of the pseudobulbs. They are 1 inch (2.5 cm) across, distinctly mottled with glossy dark red markings, and have a rocking lip.

Cultivation

Mount this species on bark or tree-fern slab, ensuring high humidity and good air circulation. Generous watering is required with a weekly application of weak fertilizer. Intermediate to warm temperatures (summer daytime 68 to 77°F/20 to 25°C, nighttime 64 to 68°F/18 to 20°C, lower in winter) are needed, as well as bright light with dappled shade.

Classification

Bulbophyllum frostii Summerhayes 1928.

Bulbophyllum frostii

Bulbophyllum grandiflorum

Occurring from Malaysia to the Solomon Islands, *Bulbophyllum grandiflorum* grows epiphytically on shrubs and trees. The 2-inch- (5-cm-) long pseudobulbs are topped with a single 6-in- (15-cm-) long paddle-shaped leaf and are widely spaced on a creeping rhizome. *Bulbophyllum grandiflorum* has a very unusual flower, reminiscent of a crested bird's head and measuring 4 inches (10 cm) across. Flowers are greenish yellow and mottled brown in color. Throughout the summer numerous single flowers are produced, falling from the base of the pseudobulbs and from along the rhizome.

Cultivation

Bulbophyllum grandiflorum is happy to be mounted on tree-fern slabs or bark but can also be grown in a basket with a small amount of medium consisting of osmunda fiber or a sphagnum moss mix. It requires warm to intermediate temperatures (summer daytime 68 to 77°F/20 to 25°C, nighttime 64–68°F/ 18–20°C, lower in winter) with a good circulation of air and high humidity. Generous watering is required, but a slight drying between watering will prevent rotting. Weekly applications of weak fertilizer are needed, as is low indirect light.

Classification

Bulbophyllum grandiflorum Blume 1849.

Bulbophyllum grandiflorum

Bulbophyllum lobbii

This variable species is found from Thailand to Malaysia, Indonesia, and the Philippines at elevations between 3,300 and 6,000 feet (1,000–1,800 m).

The pseudobulbs grow along a creeping rhizome, spaced at up to 3.25 inches (8 cm) apart and are 3 inches (7.5 cm) long, each topped by a paddle-shaped leathery leaf that is up to 10 inches (25 cm) long.

Bulbophyllum lobbii flowers measure about 2.4 inches (6 cm) across and arise from a 4-inch- (10-cm-) long scape. Their color ranges from buttery cream to a deep yellow with stripes of reddish brown. They bloom from late spring to summer and are very fragrant.

Cultivation

This species likes to grow in a shallow pan or pot with little growing medium (osmunda fiber or sphagnum moss mix). Alternatively, it can be mounted on bark or tree-fern slabs. Water generously and maintain high humidity and a good circulation of air. Warm to intermediate temperatures (summer daytime 68 to 77°F/ 20 to 25°C, nighttime 64 to 68°F/18 to 20°C, lower in winter) are required with dappled shade. Regular weekly applications with weak fertilizer are needed during the growing season. Although it is a relatively easy plant to grow, it is susceptible to fungal rot if kept too wet.

Classification

Bulbophyllum lobbii Lindley 1847.

Bulbophyllum lobbii

Bulbophyllum medusae

From Thailand to western Malaysia, *Bulbophyllum medusae* can be found growing as an epiphyte dangling from trees or occasionally as a lithophyte on rocks. The species epithet alludes to the long lateral sepals that resemble the snakes on the head of the Greek mythological figure Medusa.

The pseudobulbs are conical, angled, often yellowish, 1.5 inches (4 cm) tall, and borne on a stout rhizome. Each pseudobulb carries a single leaf, which is rigid and leathery and measures 8 inches (20 cm) long and 2 inches (5 cm) wide. The leaves have a short stalk at the base and are oblong, with a blunt and slightly cleft apex.

The flowers are clustered like a mop head at the end of the inflorescence, which is about 8 inches (20 cm) long. The most distinctive features of the flowers are the long—up to 6 inches (15 cm)—tapering, fiberlike, cream sepals which are sometimes spotted red.

Cultivation

In order to display the unusual dangling clusters of flowers at their best, this plant should be grown mounted on bark or tree-fern slabs. It can tolerate drought and lower temperatures but will flower readily if kept at the warm to intermediate range of temperatures. Water well, then allow it to dry out between watering. An application of weak fertilizer every two weeks, moderate humidity, and a good circulation of air are required.

Classification

Bulbophyllum medusae (Lindley) Reichenbach f. 1861.

Bulbophyllum medusae

Other *Bulbophyllum* Species

Bulbophyllum makoyanum from Singapore, Borneo, and the Philippines.

Bulbophyllum carunculatum from the Philippines.

Overleaf: *Bulbophyllum rothschildianum* from India.

Bulbophyllum odoratum
from Malesia.

*Bulbophyllum
longiflorum* from
East Africa to the Pacific.

*Bulbophyllum
kanburiense*
from Indochina.

Bulbophyllum mirum from
Thailand to Malesia.

*Bulbophyllum
unitubum* from
New Guinea.

Bulbophyllum Hybrids

Bulbophyllum 'Elizabeth Ann Buckleberry'   *Bulbophyllum* 'Louis Sander'

*Bulbophyllum
graveolens* 'Vera Cruz'

Calanthe

Number of Species: About 200.

Classification: *Calanthe* R. Brown 1821; tribe Arethuseae, subtribe Bletiinae.

Form: This genus comprises deciduous and evergreen terrestrial orchids with ovate, plicate leaves growing up to 24 in (60 cm) long. The inflorescence is a raceme that can grow up to 36 in (91 cm) tall. It is densely covered with small to medium flowers with a three- or four-lobed lip fused at the base and sometimes forming a spur.

Distribution: Tropical and subtropical Africa, Asia, and Australia.

Habitat: Grows in shaded and semishaded conditions with moisture-retentive but not boggy or waterlogged soil.

The name *Calanthe* is from the Greek *kalos* ("beautiful") and *anthos* ("flower"). The genus is allied to *Phaius*. This genus was used to create the first man-made orchid hybrid ('Calanthe Dominii') in 1853.

This medium to large terrestrial genus is divided into two groups. Some are deciduous and others are evergreen, keeping their leaves for several seasons. The evergreen species are the hardiest, some withstanding temperatures as low as 14°F (-10°C) and a covering of snow. *Calanthe tricarinata* is a medium-sized, very hardy species with extremely beautiful 1- to 2-inch (2.5–5-cm) apple green flowers with contrasting red lips.

The deciduous *Calanthe* species are native to warm Asian forests, where a wet spring and summer and a dry fall and winter are experienced. They grow terrestrially in deep patches of forest humus, on rotting logs and among rocks with crevices filled with leaf litter.

Cultivation

Hardy evergreen *Calanthe* species, typically from temperate Japanese and Chinese woodlands, require a compost of one-quarter very fine composted bark, one-quarter mature sifted compost, one-quarter organic peat (or peat-free equivalent), and one-quarter sharp sand or grit for good drainage.

They should never be allowed to dry out completely—the compost should be constantly moist but never wet. Apply fertilizer only during the growing season with one-quarter to one-half strength balanced fertilizer every week. Never apply fertilizer to a dry plant—always ensure it is watered first before applying any fertilizer.

Calanthe sieboldii var. *kawakamii* 'Good Fortune'

Different hardy evergreen species and hybrids are hardy to different temperatures; all except *C. izu-insularis* are hardy to below 32°F (0°C). *Calanthe tricarinata* resents high temperatures and should not be exposed to temperatures above 77°F (25°C) for extended periods.

Deciduous *Calanthe* species require a potting medium of one-quarter sifted fine compost, one-quarter perlite, one-quarter sphagnum moss, and one-quarter composted cow or sheep manure (heat-treated composted farm yard manure is fine). When repotting deciduous *Calanthe*, separate the pseudobulbs out to single bulbs, leaving on the old roots, which are not alive at this stage. Bury the roots, keeping the pseudobulb level with the medium because the bulbs are prone to rotting. Do not be tempted to water at this stage; simply place on a bright windowsill or bench and wait for new growth. Once the new growth is up to about 6 inches (15 cm), roots will emerge from the bottom of the pseudobulb, and watering can be resumed.

Temperature ranges from 55 to 85°F (13–29°C), with high humidity and a good air circulation, are required. Apply fertilizer every two to three weeks during the growing season and do not allow the medium to dry out completely at this time. When the leaves begin to yellow in the fall, reduce water to allow the plants to dry between watering. The leaves will wither and die, but keep the plants in humid conditions, with occasional light watering to ensure the top of the potting medium stays damp. The flower stems will then appear and will bloom for several weeks to a few months. Once blooming is over and new growths appear, divide the bulbs and repot as before.

Calanthe vestita is a deciduous species from Thailand and Myanmar and has pink or white flowers.

Calanthe puberula

Occurring in the northwest Himalayas, India, eastward to China, Japan, and Taiwan, *Calanthe puberula* grows to altitudes of 4,265 to 8,200 feet (1,300–2,500 m) and flowers from July to September. Plants are evergreen, 8 to 20 inches (20–50 cm) tall with three to six oblanceolate to linear leaves up to 12 inches (30 cm) long. The racemes carry up to 30 flowers, 0.8 inch (2 cm) in diameter, which vary in color from white to lilac. The lip is three-lobed and lacks a spur.

Cultivation

As a hardy evergreen, *C. puberula* requires a compost of one-quarter very fine composted bark, one-quarter mature sifted compost, one-quarter organic peat (or peat-free equivalent) and one-quarter sharp sand or grit for good drainage. It should never be allowed to dry out completely—the compost should be constantly moist but never wet. Apply fertilizer only during the growing season with one-quarter to one-half strength balanced fertilizer every week. Never apply fertilizer to a dry plant— always ensure it is watered first before applying any fertilizer. *Calanthe puberula* should be grown at intermediate temperatures.

Classification

Calanthe puberula var. *reflexa* Lindley 1833.

Calanthe puberula

Calanthe triplicata

Often found in very shaded moist gullies in rain forests, *Calanthe triplicata* occurs in New Guinea, Sri Lanka, India, and China. It is also the only member of *Calanthe* to occur in Australia, where it is popularly known as the Christmas Orchid, since it flowers from late November to the end of January.

This species is a beautiful, highly variable evergreen orchid. It can be, as in Australia, a large species with three or four large pleated leaves up to 36 inches (91 cm) long and 7 inches (18 cm) wide. The inflorescence can be over 39 inches (100 cm) high with numerous 1-inch (2.5-cm) white flowers densely packed at the top of the spike with a lip resembling a Lorraine cross. The more compact Chinese form has a rosette of 6- to 8-inch- (15–20-cm-) long pleated leaves with 18-inch (45-cm-) high erect flower spikes topped with a dense head of pure white blooms, 1 inch (2.5 cm) wide.

The flowers are very delicate and will mark if handled; this is caused by the release of the chemical indican, which is the same as contained in the dye woad.

Cultivation
Calanthe triplicata is one of the easier orchids to grow. It can be grown in the garden in a very shaded and well-drained area that can be kept moist in drier times; some protection from frost is needed. In a greenhouse, plant in a large pot containing a compost of one-quarter very fine composted bark, one-quarter mature sifted compost, one-quarter organic peat (or peat-free equivalent) and one-quarter sharp sand or grit for good drainage. They should never be allowed to dry out completely - the compost should be constantly moist but never wet. Apply fertilizer only during the growing season with one-quarter to one-half strength balanced fertilizer every week. Never apply fertilizer to a dry plant—always ensure it is watered first before applying any fertilizer.

Classification
Calanthe triplicata (Willemet) Ames, Philipp. J. 1907.

Calanthe triplicata

Catasetum

DATA

Number of Species: About 180.

Classification: *Catasetum*
L. C. Richard ex Kunth 1822;
tribe Cymbidieae, subtribe
Catasetinae.

Form: This genus has fleshy cigar-shaped pseudobulbs with several long internodes. The eight to 12 leaves are pleated in the upper part and deciduous. The pseudobulbs become spiny after their leaves are shed. The flowering stem carries few to many flowers and emerges from the base of the pseudobulbs.

Distribution: From the West Indies to Mexico in Central America and to Argentina in South America; the majority of species are found in Brazil.

Habitat: These epiphytes are found in a wide variety of habitats including deciduous forests, grasslands, coastal regions, and lowland tropical forests to elevations of 4,000–5,000 ft (1,200–1,500 m).

The name *Catasetum*, from the Greek *kata* ("down") and the Latin *seta* ("bristle"), refers to the two antenna-like appendages at the base of the column of male flowers. All *Catasetum* species have separate male and female flowers, usually borne on separate inflorescences. The flowers are highly fragrant and of a fleshy texture. Male flowers are very colorful, while the female flowers are usually yellowish green.

The two antennae at the base of the column in male (staminate) flowers are sensitive, explosively releasing the pollinia on touch. There are fewer female (pistillate) flowers. The helmet-shaped or saccate lip of each flower often consists of three lobes. The column is very short. The sex of the flowers depends on the conditions in which they were grown; female flowers will often be produced under conditions of high light and low moisture, whilst male flowers are produced in a shadier situation with higher moisture. In very rare cases a single plant grown in intermediate conditions may produce both male and female flowers.

Cultivation

Catasetum species should be grown in open baskets containing sphagnum moss or mounted on tree-fern slabs or on bark with sphagnum moss around the roots. They need heavy feeding (composted horse manure with charcoal or cow or sheep manure mixes have been used in days gone by) and copious watering when in active growth, with frequent applications of dilute fertilizer. A good circulation of air and moderate humidity are required, with intermediate to warm temperatures during the growth period. The plants should be repotted or remounted each year for best growth, dividing to a single pseudobulb.

Catasetum pileatum is found from Trinidad to Ecuador.

Catasetum saccatum

This orchid grows in galleried forests in Peru, Colombia, Ecuador, Venezuela, and Brazil at 650 to 5,600 feet (200–1,700 m). Its fusiform, elongate pseudobulbs bear four to seven elliptic-lanceolate leaves. Sepals and petals may be green or dark brown and are always mottled. The lip margins are dentate or fringed with long hairs or threadlike outgrowths. The long arching inflorescence can carry 30 flowers, each up to 4 inches (10 cm) across.

Cultivation

Strong but indirect light is needed, with good air circulation and high humidity. Grow in open baskets filled with sphagnum moss or mounted on tree-fern slabs or bark with sphagnum moss around the roots. Grow at intermediate to warm temperatures; water and feed generously until the leaves drop, and reduce watering in winter. If temperatures drop below 70°F (21°C), reduce watering further. Repot or remount every year when the first new shoots appear.

Classification

Catasetum saccatum Lindley 1840.

Catasetum saccatum

Catasetum tenebrosum

This cool-growing species occurs in Peru and Ecuador at altitudes of 4,000 to 6,200 feet (1,200–1,900 m) and in similar zones in parts of western Brazil. Typically the habitat is on exposed Andean slopes where the plants may be in direct sunlight, but where cooling winds and breezes keep them from burning. This species' epithet comes from the Latin word *tenebrosus*, meaning "dark"—a reference to the color of the sepals. The beautiful, almost black, flowers have a yellow lip that exposes the stamen, which has a cartridge-case ejection mechanism to scatter the pollinia.

Cultivation

Because *Catasetum tenebrosum* comes from a cold climate and becomes dormant in the winter, it can be cultivated in similar climates. The natural cooling breezes of its natural environment cannot be mimicked in the greenhouse, so this species must be grown in dappled light. It prefers a hanging basket (high up in the greenhouse) filled with sphagnum moss; alternatively, it can be mounted on tree-fern slabs or on bark with sphagnum around the roots.

There needs to be a distinct difference in the watering regime between its growing season and its dormant period. Water is critical for producing large pseudobulbs (which see the plant through its dormancy) and strong flower growth. Water heavily, with weekly fertilizer applications while the leaves are forming, especially when flower spikes are appearing. During hot summers, mist the leaves to stop them from shriveling. Reduce watering when the leaves start to yellow and when the plant stops flowering.

Once the leaves have fallen off, keep the plant dry for the duration of the dormant period. Good circulation of air is essential because this species is prone to bulb rot. High humidity and generous watering and feeding are essential during the growing season.

Classification

Catasetum tenebrosum Kraenzlin 1910.

Catasetum tenebrosum

Cattleya

DATA

Number of Species: About 40.

Classification: *Cattleya* Lindley 1824; tribe Epidendreae, subtribe Laeliinae.

Form: Pseudobulbs are cylindrical, 6 to 32 in (15–81 cm) long, and protected by straw-colored papery sheaths. Leaves are apical and thick. Inflorescence is racemose with a sheath at the base and carries up to four showy flowers. Flowers are fragrant and appear in a range of colors (typically purple). They are often blotched or spotted and measure 2 to 5 in (10–13 cm) across. They have two fringed petals and one with a conspicuous lip. There are four club-shaped (clavate) pollinia.

Distribution: Throughout the American tropics, the main diversity being in coastal Brazil and the Andes.

Habitat: Grow as epiphytes in moist tropical forests, often in treetops where the roots can be seen dangling below branches.

The genus *Cattleya* is well known for its large showy flowers. Its species, hybrids, and cultivars have dominated the orchid cut-flower and houseplant market for a century. The genus was named by John Lindley in 1824 for William Cattley, an ardent collector of exotic plants. Cattley had originally received the plants as protective packing for other exotics. Their leathery leaves and pseudobulbs attracted his attention and he duly potted them up with the rest of his consignment, placed them in a hot and humid environment, and waited. Within a few months he was rewarded with beautiful pale lilac flowers with a subtle fragrance.

Taxonomy

Two forms of *Cattleya* exist. Bifoliates (from the Amazon and eastern Brazil) have pseudobulbs with two leaves and numerous small flowers. Their texture is firm and the lip is relatively small. Monofoliates (from Brazil, Colombia, Panama, Peru, and Venezuela) have a single leaf, larger flowers, and a larger lip. As a result of DNA studies, some species of *Cattleya* have recently been moved to *Cattleyella* and *Guarianthe*.

Natural hybrids occur between various *Cattleya* species and between *Cattleya* species and members of other genera (see Table overleaf). This proclivity to hybridization has been greatly extended by horticulturalists, using related genera such as *Laelia*, *Brassavola*, and *Sophronitis*.

Combinations of genera have produced some wonderful hybrids, with a variety of colors through the spectrum, the exception being true blue. In addition, thousands of named cultivars have been bred. This whole grouping of genera, species, intergeneric and intrageneric hybrids, and cultivars is often refered to as the "Cattleya Alliance."

The spring-flowering *Cattleya lueddemanniana* is a native of Venezuela.

Cultivation

Cattleyas appreciate heat, humidity, and a well-drained potting medium such as fine bark or a mix of perlite, bark, and sphagnum moss. Humidity can be maintained by placing the pots on trays of gravel partially filled with water. They like to dry out between watering, and good air circulation is essential to prevent disease. Misting them in the morning is beneficial in dry climates. For mature plants a temperature variation of 10 to 20°F (6–12°C) from day to night seems beneficial, with the daytime temperature being higher, at 70 to 85°F (21–29° C).

During active growth *Cattleya* species need a high-nitrogen fertilizer every two weeks, and every month when not growing. To promote healthy blooms, use a high-phosphorus blooming booster every four to six applications. Repot after flowering or in spring and/or when the rhizome starts to protrude out of the pot and before new roots appear.

Cattleya (Guarianthe) bowringiana occurs in Honduras and Guatemala.

Examples of *Cattleya* Hybrid Alliance

Brassavola x *Cattleya* = x *Brassocattleya* (Bc.)
Brassavola x *Laelia* x *Cattleya* = x *Brassolaeliocattleya* (Blc.)
Laelia x *Cattleya* = x *Laeliocattleya* (Lc.)
Brassavola x *Laelia* x *Sophronitis* x *Cattleya* = x *Potinara* (Pot.)
Sophronitis x *Cattleya* = x *Sophrocattleya* (Sc.)
Sophronitis x *Laelia* x *Cattleya* = x *Sophrolaeliocattleya* (Slc.)

Abbreviations in brackets are accepted shortened forms for the hybrid.

Cattleya leopoldii (tigrina)

This Brazilian coastal species is closely related to *Cattleya guttata*, of which it has sometimes been regarded as a form. However, *C. guttata* occurs farther north than *C. leopoldii*, and their distributions do not overlap. *Cattleya leopoldii* is itself often now regarded by some authorities as part of *C. tigrina*. In the wild *C. leopoldii* naturally hydridizes with a number of other orchids, the best-known example being with *Laelia purpurata* (*L. elegans*)—the result is *Laeliocattleya elegans,* a very variable and widespread form.

Cattleya leopoldii is an epiphyte and has elongated, canelike pseudobulbs that bear a pair of leaves at the apex. The inflorescence can carry up to 20 flowers. These are always reddish brown or very dark maroon with dark maroon or dark red, almost chocolate-colored markings. *Cattleya leopoldii* has a wide, spreading, velvety purple lip.

This species inhabits the Brazilian coastal plains of states from São Paulo to Rio Grande do Sul. They are most often found on beach sand dunes (where they are usually attached to shrubs) or on coastal swamp trees. Their flowering season is November to January.

Cultivation

Cattleya leopoldii requires warm temperatures and should be planted in medium-sized bark orchid compost. It is best placed in a high light situation and should be fed regularly during the growing period.

Classification

Cattleya leopoldii Verschaft 1854; *Cattleya tigrina* A. Richard 1848.

Cattleya leopoldii

Cattleya walkeriana

One of the most widespread *Cattleya* species, *C. walkeriana* might well be the most common orchid in its Brazilian habitat. It can grow in considerable numbers and often produces large clumps.

Cattleya walkeriana is largely epiphytic on trees but is also lithophytic on rocks. The plants are small—roughly 4 inches (10 cm) in height—and bear a single fleshy leaf up to 4.75 inches (12 cm) long. An inflorescence, borne on top of an elongated club-shaped pseudobulb, has up to three flowers.

The flowers are 4 inches (10 cm) across and vary in color from pink or purple to lilac. There is also an *alba* (white) form. This species is a favorite among growers because of the large flowers produced on such small plants. It has been also been used extensively for hybridizing.

Cattleya walkeriana has a large distribution, mainly in the state of Minas Gerais, Brazil. To the west, the area extends well into the states of Mato Grosso and Goiás, reaching north up to the Distrito Federal near Brasilia.

In the east, it inhabits the seasonally dry zone behind the mountain ranges of the coast, and to the west its distribution is limited by the extremely dry central area of Brazil. The very long dry period (fall to winter) lasts three to six months, depending on particular location. The plants grow in roughly equal numbers on deciduous trees (which loose their leaves in the dry period) and directly attached to rocks. These growing conditions allow the plants to receive almost full sunlight during the cooler and dryer season but with shade from foliage during the hot wet season.

Cultivation

It grows well in warm, high light situations in sphagnum moss or medium bark, either in a pot or mounted on bark with a little sphagnum moss to cling to. It should be fed regularly during the growing period.

Classification

Cattleya walkeriana Gardner 1843.

Cattleya walkeriana

Other *Cattleya* Species

Cattleya trianae from Colombia.

Cattleya schilleriana from Brazil.

Cattleya iricolor from
Ecuador to Peru.

Cattleya forbesii
from Brazil.

Hybrids Involving *Cattleya*

Cattleya 'Carousel Crimson'

x *Laeliocattleya* 'Drumbeat Heritage'

Cattleya 'Desmond'

x *Brassolaeliocattleya* 'Bric de Valec'

Cattleya 'Virtue'

x *Brassocattleya* High Sierra 'Lynn'

x *Brassocattleya* 'Binosa'

x *Brassolaeliocattleya* 'Elizabeth Hearn'

x *Epicattleya* Fireball 'Royal Orange'

Brassolaeliocattleya
yce Canyon 'Splendiferous'

CATTLEYA

x *Laeliocattleya*
'El Cerrito'

x *Laeliocattleya* 'Loog Tone'

x *Laeliocattleya* 'Remula'

x *Potinara*
'Susan Fender'

x *Potinara* Free Spirit 'Doc'

x *Sophrocattleya* 'Royal Bea

x *Sophrolaeliocattleya* Hazel Boyd 'Sunset'

x *Sophrolaeliocattleya* Hazel Boyd 'Red Stone'

x *Sophrolaeliocattleya* Little Fairy 'Flower Ball'

Chysis

Number of Species: About 9.

Classification: *Chysis* Lindley 1837; tribe Epidendreae, subtribe Bletiinae.

Form: Fleshy, pendent, elongated pseudobulbs with thin, strongly veined, soft, papery leaves that are semideciduous, often being retained for two years. The multi-flowered inflorescence emanates with new growth from the base of the pseudobulb. The pollinia are soft and mealy (powdery).

Distribution: From Mexico south to Peru and east to Andean Venezuela.

Habitat: Epiphytes found in wet shady forests from elevations of 1,600 to 3,250 feet (490 to 990 m).

The inflorescences of *Chysis* species are multiflowered and emanate from the base of the pseudobulbs with new growth. Flower colors range from white to orangish yellow. Flowers are fragrant and long-lasting, and some species are self-pollinating.

Chysis aurea, from Venezuela, Colombia, and possibly northward to Panama, has wavy, rather soft-textured, strongly ribbed leaves up to 12 inches (30 cm) long and about 2 inches (5 cm) wide. Some orchid authorities consider *C. aurea* and *C. laevis* to be synonymous and have classified them both as *C. aurea* with distribution from Mexico through Central America to Venezuela, Colombia, and Peru. Most specialists, however, now consider plants from Mexico and northern Central America to be *C. laevis* and plants from South America *C. aurea*.

Cultivation

Members of this genus are best grown mounted on bark, small branches, or tree-fern slabs (because of their pendulous habit) with sphagnum moss around the roots to retain moisture. Heavy watering and weekly feeding (one-quarter to one-half recommended strength) are required during the growing season with a good circulation of air and high humidity (75 to 80 percent all year round). Water should be reduced in late fall and winter after new growths have matured, but do not allow plants to remain dry for long periods. Fertilizer should be reduced or eliminated until new growth starts and heavier watering is resumed in spring. Intermediate temperatures (summer daytime 68 to 77°F/20 to 25°C, nighttime 64 to 68°F/18 to 20°C, lower in winter) are required.

Chysis aurea is one of the yellow-flowered members of the genus.

Cochlioda

DATA

Number of Species: About 6.

Classification: *Cochlioda* Lindley 1853; tribe Cymbidieae, subtribe Oncidiinae.

Form: From small to medium epiphytic (some lithophytic) orchids, with a short creeping rhizome. Pseudobulbs are short, unifoliate, or bifoliate at apex, wrinkling with age. Leaves are linear to oblong, 8 in (20 cm) long, and dark green. One or two racemose, slender, and arching inflorescences up to 18 in (45 cm) long are produced. The often numerous flowers are small to medium, scarlet or rose red in color. The sepals are free, not quite equal, while the petals are spreading and oblique. The lip is three-lobed, with the lateral lobes rounded. The column is slender, winged above, and bears two pollinia.

Distribution: Peru, Bolivia, Ecuador.

Habitat: Cloud forest up to 10,500 ft (3,200 m).

Cochliodas are renowned for their numerous flowers, which are carried in graceful sprays on slender spikes that emerge from the base of the pseudobulbs. The name cochlioda derives from the Greek word for "spiral"—*kochlion*—a reference to the shape of the callus on the lip, which resembles a snail shell. The type species was described in 1853 as *C. densiflora* by John Lindley, from a collection obtained by A. Mathews while in Peru.

Cochlioda species have been used in hybridizing with related genera including *Oncidium*, *Odontoglossum*, and *Miltonia*. They are also involved in many popular intergeneric hybrids, for example, the bigeneric hybrids x *Miltonioda*, x *Oncidioda*, and x *Odontioda* and the trigeneric and quadrigeneric hybrids, such as x *Wilsonara*, x *Vuylstekeara*, and x *Burrageara*.

Cultivation

These orchids grow well in pots with well-drained medium or sphagnum moss. Since members of this genus grow at high altitudes they require cool growing conditions (summer daytime 61°F/16°C, night 55°F/13°C, and winter daytime 55°F/13°C, night 50°F/10°C). Grow in shady, conditions with good fresh air circulation and with moderate humidity. Keep moist at all times. Increase watering when new growth appears and reduce once the growth is complete. The hybrids are somewhat more adaptable to varying conditions.

Cochlioda rosea occurs from Ecuador to Peru.

Cochlioda noezliana

Occurring in the cloud forests of Bolivia and Peru at elevations of 6,500 to 11,500 feet (2,000–3,500 m) *Cochlioda noezliana* grows in shady conditions. Its pseudobulbs are compressed laterally, ovoid, and wrinkle with age. The leaves are solitary, obtuse, and 10 inches (25 cm) long. The inflorescence is up to 18 inches (45 cm) long, arching, and bears many vivid scarlet flowers with a golden yellow disk on the callus of the lip and a violet purple column. The flowers are spreading and open widely, reaching 2 inches (5 cm) across. They appear in the summer and fall. The lip is three-lobed, the lateral lobes being rounded.

Cultivation

Cochlioda noezliana was one of the last species of the genus to be discovered and cultivated (in 1891). It grows well in pots with well-drained medium or sphagnum moss. It requires cool growing conditions (summer daytime 61°F/16°C, night 55°F/13°C; winter daytime 55°F/13°C, night 50°F/10°C). Grow in shady conditions with good fresh air circulation and moderate humidity. Keep moist at all times. Increase watering when new growth appears and reduce the amount of water given once the growth is complete.

Classification

Cochlioda noezliana (Masters ex L. Linden) Rolfe 1891.

Cochlioda noezliana

Coelogyne

DATA

Number of Species: About 150.

Classification: *Coelogyne* Lindley 1821; tribe Coelogyneae, subtribe Coelogyninae (several type species were cited by John Lindley when establishing the genus).

Form: Epiphytic plants with a short or long rhizome. The pseudobulbs are ovoid, conical, or cylindrical, clustered together or well spaced, bearing one or two leaves. Leaves are apical, rarely basal, elliptical to lanceolate, plicate.

Distribution: Southeast Asia, India, Malaysia, Indonesia, China, Pacific islands.

Habitat: By sides of running streams to high up in the branches of trees in lowland forests. Some can be found as terrestrials growing on limestone.

The Greek word *koilos* means "hollow" and *gyne* means "woman." This is how the genus came to be named Coelogyne—it aptly describes the deep stigmatic cavity that is characteristic of the genus. *Coelogyne* species are relatively easy to grow and they produce long-lasting fragrant flowers. They have never become really popular with growers and have been generally ignored by hybridizers over the years. In the 1970s, *C. mooreana* was crossed with *C. cristata* to produce *Coelogyne* 'Linda Buckley.'

The inflorescence is an erect or pendulous, terminal raceme carrying many flowers. The flowers are showy, small to large, with free, often concave, sepals. The petals are free and narrower than the sepals. The lip is three-lobed. The column bears two long pollinia.

Cultivation

Coelogynes come from a wide range of habitats with a temperature range of cold to hot and everything in between. It is therefore critical to know exactly which species is being grown in order to replicate the growing conditions accurately. Those with a good spreading rhizome are best placed on a piece of bark or in a hanging basket. Those that require higher temperatures and high humidity are best contained within pots. Clay pots tend to keep the roots cooler and moist. Bright but shaded light is essential. Look to see where a plant is from and then fit it into a pot or basket. Those from cooler temperatures also require a rest period and like to be kept dry at this time, with just a light misting.

Coelogyne usitana is endemic to the small island of Mindanao in the Philippines.

Coelogyne cristata

This species occurs on trees and rocks in moss forests at altitudes of 5,250 to 8,500 feet (1,600–2,600 m) in the Himalayas of northern India across to Nepal and northern Thailand. Its clustered pseudobulbs are oblong to round and bear two narrow lanceolate leaves up to 12 inches (30 cm) long. The inflorescence is a pendent raceme, producing three to 10 flowers that can be fragrant. They are 3 inches (8 cm) across and have similar white sepals and petals. The three-lobed lip is white with yellow to orange lamellae.

Cultivation

As a species from the Himalayas growing in mist and fog, *Coelogyne cristata* requires cool conditions but high light levels. Grow in pans or baskets, with well-drained sphagnum moss, maintaining fresh air movement and intermediate to high humidity. It should be watered heavily while actively growing, with little if any drying allowed between waterings. Water should then be gradually reduced after new growths have matured in the fall, and limited in winter to occasional light waterings or early morning mistings. A balanced fertilizer mixed at one-quarter to-one-half the recommended strength should be applied weekly during periods of active growth.

Classification

Coelogyne cristata Lindley 1824.

Coelogyne cristata

Coelogyne fimbriata

This widespread species occurs from sea level to 4,500 feet (1,400 m) in India, Nepal, China, Vietnam, and the Malay Peninsula. Its pseudobulbs grow from a slender creeping rhizome and are ovoid to ellipsoid, with one to three apical leaves. The leaves are oblong to elliptic, 3.5 inches (9 cm) long, and acute. The erect inflorescence is 2 inches (5 cm) tall, with papery sheaths at the base. The 1- to 2- inch (2.5–5-cm) flowers are long lasting with a sweet musky scent. Sepals and petals are pale yellow. The three-lobed lip is whitish to pale yellow in color, with a dark brown fringed margin. The disk is keeled, the two outer keels being undulate to the center of the midlobe, and flanked by two short keels.

Cultivation

Coelogyne fimbriata can be grown under cool to warm temperature regimes. Strong air movement and high humidity with strong but shaded light are important. This species requires only a short rest period, but must be kept moist at this time.

Classification

Coelogyne fimbriata Lindley 1825.

Coelogyne fimbriata

Coelogyne mooreana

A native of Vietnam, *Coelogyne mooreana* grows in cloud forests at altitudes up to 3,900 feet (1,200 m) in the Lang Bien Mountains. It is an epiphyte that grows 12 to 18 inches (30–45 cm) tall. Pseudobulbs are clustered, ovoid, and lightly furrowed. The leaves are linear to oblanceolate, acute, and up to 16 inches (40 cm) long. The inflorescence is 15 to 20 inches (38–50 cm) tall and bears four to eight erect white flowers, 3 to 4 inches (7.5–10 cm) across. Petals and sepals are similar, broadly lanceolate in shape. The white lip is three-lobed and has an orange or ocher-colored disk. The column is long.

Cultivation

Strong air movement and high humidity are critical at all times. While strong sunlight is important, shading is needed from spring through fall. Temperature requirements are in the range of cool to warm. In the wild, summer days average 77 to 78°F (25–26°C), and nights average 62°F (17°C). The warmest days occur in spring, when daytime temperatures average 81 to 82°F (27–28°C). During the winter rest period, days average 76 to 79°F (25–26°C), while nighttime temperatures fall to 53 to 55°F (12–13°C).

Water heavily while the plant is actively growing, but little or no drying should be allowed between waterings. Water should be gradually reduced after new growths have matured in the fall and limited in winter to occasional light waterings or early morning mistings. A balanced fertilizer mixed at one-quarter to one-half recommended strength should be applied weekly during periods of active growth. The flowers can last in good condition for four to six weeks if kept cool.

Classification

Coelogyne mooreana Rolfe 1907.

Coelogyne mooreana

144

Coelogyne rochusseni

High up in the tree canopy in the forests of Malaysia, Indonesia, Thailand, and the Philippines, the pendulous clusters of yellow flowers of *Coelogyne rochusseni* form a stunning site virtually all year round. This orchid can be found at altitudes from sea level to 4,900 feet (1,500 m). Its narrow, grooved pseudobulbs are spaced along a rhizome. The two leaves emerging from each pseudobulb are oblanceolate to obovate and up to 12 inches (30 cm) long. The inflorescence emerges from near the base of old pseudobulbs, It is up to 28 inches (71 cm) long, slender, pendent, and bears up to 40 fragrant flowers.

The flowers are lemon yellow; the sepals are narrowly lanceolate, and the petals are even narrower. The lip is three-lobed, decurved, narrowing at the point, and has yellow keels and striped brown lateral lobes. The flowers tend to half close at night and reopen with the sun.

Cultivation

Because of its forest canopy habitat this species is best displayed in a hanging basket or on a cork bark raft to fully reveal its pendulous flower clusters. It requires good light, free air circulation, and high humidity. Like all coelogynes, it does not like disturbance at the roots.

Classification

Coelogyne rochusseni De Vriese 1854.

Coelogyne rochusseni

Other *Coelogyne* Species

Coelogyne flaccida
from India, Nepal,
and southern China.

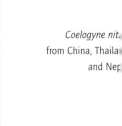

Coelogyne mayeriana
from the Malay Peninsula
and Sumatra.

Coelogyne nit
from China, Thaila
and Nep

Coryanthes

Number of Species: About 30.

Classification: *Coryanthes* Hooker 1831; tribe Cymbidieae, subtribe Stanhopeinae.

Form: Large epiphytic orchids with a short stout rhizome. The fleshy pseudobulbs are glossy dark green, short to elongated, becoming ridged with age, and bear two or three leaves. The leaves are apical, large, folded, and veined on the underside. The racemose arching to pendulous inflorescence appears from base of the pseudobulb and bears a few flowers.

Distribution: Central to South America, Guatemala, Peru, Brazil, Colombia, West Indies.

Habitat: Grow on trees within lowland forests in very wet conditions at altitudes up to 3,200 ft (975 m). They tend to be sited on the outside of branches to catch good light.

The flowers of *Coryanthes* species are large, showy, and waxy and have a complex structure. The sepals are free, broadly elliptical, with the dorsal sepal shorter than the lateral sepals. The petals are erect, twisted, and smaller than the sepals. The lip is pendent and spreading. The hypochile forms an upside-down helmet shape, the mesochile is elongate and tubelike, and the epichile is large. The column is long, tapering to a point, with two wings or horns at its base. There are two waxy pollinia.

Bees of the genera *Euglossa*, *Euplusia*, and *Eulaemia* are thought to be the main pollinators of this orchid. A sticky secretion within the epichile makes it hard for a bee to escape; when it does it must climb the tunnel between the epichile and the column, brushing against the pollinium and removing it on its back. Visiting the next flower, it deposits the pollinium as it squeezes between the stigma and anther.

The root system of *Coryanthes* is usually located within an ant's nest. Ant species of the genera *Camponutus* and *Azteca* build their nests around the roots, but how this benefits the plant or the ant is not known. Coryanthes also often grow in proximity to *Epidendrum* orchids.

Cultivation

Grow as for *Stanhopea* but with a little more heat. These orchids require copious water for most of the year with less during the rest period, but they should never be allowed to dry out. The medium needs to be well drained, more acid than alkaline, and very fertile. High humidity and moderate shade are two other requirements.

Coryanthes speciosa 'Won Hee'; in the wild this species occurs in the West Indies and Brazil.

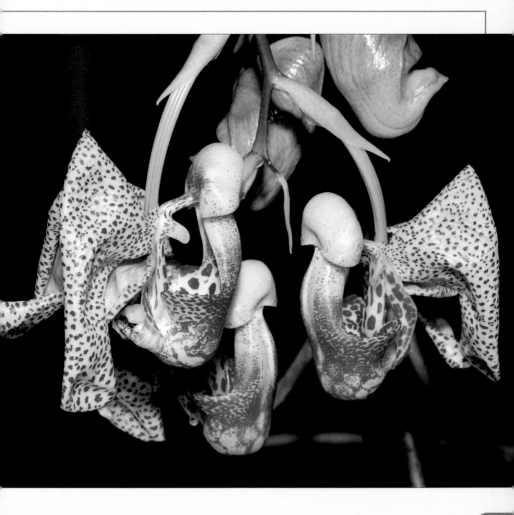

Cycnoches

DATA

Number of Species: About 23.

Classification: *Cycnoches* Lindley 1832; tribe Cymbidieae, subtribe Catasetinae.

Form: A group of epiphytic or terrestrial orchids with fleshy pseudobulbs covered in fibrous leafy sheaths. The leaves are deciduous, pleated, membranous, and heavily veined. The inflorescence is arching or pendent, carrying few to many flowers. Male and female flowers are separate and occur on the same inflorescence. Sepals and petals are somewhat similar, petals wider and spreading. The lip is crested or fringed, fleshy to thin-textured and continuous with the column base.

Distribution: Tropical America.

Habitat: Moist lowland to wet forest. Grows from sea level to 1,800 ft (550 m).

Members of the genus *Cycnoches* are known as swan orchids. The name comes from the Greek *kynos* ("swan") and *auchen* ("neck"). The long arching column of the male flowers of some species is thought to resemble a swan's neck. Some sources often spell the genus name incorrectly as "*Cynoches*."

In some species the unisexual flowers are similar, but in others they are distinctly different. In such cases the female flowers are fleshy with a club-shaped column that has three hooks at its tip. The distinctive male flowers are thinner with a long slender column. There are also fewer female than male flowers on each inflorescence. The strong fragrance of the flowers attracts particular euglossine bees; when the bees visit the male flowers the pollinia become attached to their backs and are then removed by the hooks on the column of any female flower visited.

Cultivation

Cycnoches species grow best in open baskets containing well-drained sphagnum moss or mounted on tree-fern slabs or on bark with sphagnum moss around the roots. *Cycnoches* need heavy feeding and copious watering when in active growth, with frequent applications of dilute fertilizer. Water carefully when new shoots start to grow, to allow the root system to develop. They are, however, prone to rot if overwatered. A good circulation of air and moderate humidity are required, with intermediate to warm temperatures during the growth period (daytime 80 to 100°F/27 to 38°C, nighttime 60 to 65°F/16 to 18°C, and lower once the growth is mature).

Cycnoches chlorochilon occurs from Panama to Brazil.

Cymbidiella

DATA

Number of Species: About 3.

Classification: *Cymbidiella* Rolfe 1918: tribe Cymbidieae, subtribe Cyrtopodiinae.

Form: Epiphytic or terrestrial. Elongate pseudobulbs arranged on rhizomes bearing eight to 40 leaves. Leaves are folded, fanlike, arranged in two rows, jointed at upper part of leaf sheath. The many-flowered inflorescence emerges from the base of each pseudobulb. Flowers are large, showy, yellowish green, and open widely. Sepals and petals are free or joined at the column foot. Lip is variously colored, three- to four-lobed, and lacks spur, basal callus, and lamellae. The column has a short foot, and the pollinia are attached to its base by retractile mucilaginous threads.

Distribution: Madagascar.

Habitat: Tropical rain forests with intermediate to warm temperatures and humidity.

The genus *Cymbidiella* was named as a diminutive of *Cymbidium* because it resembled members of this genus, in which it was once placed. Writing in the *Orchid Review* in 1918, Robert Allen Rolfe established *Cymbidiella* as a distinct genus. It is also allied to *Eulophiella*, *Eulophia*, and *Cymbidium*.

These orchids are confined to the wet rain forests of Madagascar at altitudes from sea level to 1,200 feet (400 m), in light but shaded conditions. They are found growing on *Raphia* palms in conjunction with the Stagshorn Fern (*Platycerium madagascariense*). This fern prefers a humidity level of 65 percent (created by daily rain followed by sun), which by inference provides ideal growing conditions for these orchids.

Cultivation

Grow in pots or baskets containing a well-drained compost such as coarse bark. Position in bright and humid situations to mimic natural conditions. If grown on rafts, a large pad of moss plus fern fiber should be used. In former times it was not unusual to mix in a little dried farmyard manure with the medium. Temperature is in the intermediate to warm range. Provide plenty of light once the pseudobulbs have completed growing, but reduce water and humidity—this will encourage flowering. Plants require minimal root disturbance, so allow them to grow into a specimen plant. Propagate by division. *Cymbidiella pardalina* grows best if placed in a basket and grown with the fern *Platycerium madagascariense*.

Cymbidiella pardalina from eastern Madagascar has 20 or more showy flowers.

Cymbidium

DATA

Number of Species: About 44.

Classification: *Cymbidium* Swartz 1799; tribe Cymbidieae, subtribe Cyrtopodiinae.

Form: Epiphytic, lithophytic, and terrestrial with prominent ovoid pseudobulbs. Leaves narrow, long, leathery, grasslike. Roots white, fleshy, branching. Pendent inflorescence is an arching raceme, erect to suberect, emerging from bulb base; bears one to many flowers. Flowers showy, with free, spreading to forward-pointing sepals and petals, which are usually similar. Lip is three–lobed, sessile, fleshy, its midlobe recurved. Column is long, with two pollinia.

Distribution: India, Southeast Asia, China, Japan, Australia.

Habitat: Broadly three groups—those from high mountainous regions grow cool in cultivation; those from lower elevations in cultivation cool to intermediate; those from tropical regions need warm temperature range.

Perhaps the most popular of orchids, *Cymbidium* species have been grown for hundreds of years as pot plants and for the cut-flower trade. The flowers are long lasting, some are fragrant, and they come in a wide range of colors including white, green, yellow, brown, pink, red, and all shades in between. Some plants can also survive temperatures as low as 45°F (7°C). Over the years thousands of hybrids have been bred and these are the plants most often seen in the flower trade.

Cultivation

The medium for *Cymbidium* species should be a moisture-retentive, free-draining compost (or, if using coarse bark, add sphagnum moss). Copious water is required during the active growing period. One-quarter strength balanced fertilizer should be applied every two weeks. In the past it was not uncommon to add a small amount of well-rotted horse manure to the mix. For the cooler group, give less water during the winter or rest period—just enough to keep the pseudobulbs plump. Warmer-growing types do not need a rest period and may be watered and fed consistently all year round.

Cymbidium species can be placed outside during warmer summer days, in a shaded spot with maybe a touch of the early sun, but not all day; return them indoors if frost is forecast. Do not move plants around too much once a flower spike is seen, since this may cause it to fail or have bud blast. Repotting can be undertaken every two to three years or as the pot becomes full with pseudobulbs—springtime is best, just as new growth starts. When repotting these plants, use two to three back bulbs with a new bulb.

Cymbidium aloifolium is widespread across India and Southeast Asia.

Cymbidium canaliculatum

Endemic to Australia, *Cymbidium canaliculatum* is found growing on trees often sited on rock faces in drier areas in Western Australia, Queensland, Northern Territory, and New South Wales. In Australia it is known as the Tiger Orchid and its collection from the wild is banned.

It is an epiphytic species and has clustered ovoid to elliptical pseudobulbs. The leaves are olive green, rigid, grooved above, and measure 6 to 20 inches (15–50 cm) long. There are one to two many-flowered inflorescences per pseudobulb. Flowers are up to 2 inches (5 cm) across, greenish brown on the underside, and olive green to bronze with longitudinal lines or spots of maroon on the topside. The sepals are spreading, oblong to elliptical; the petals are elliptic to lanceolate. The lip is ovate, 0.75 inches (2 cm) long, three-lobed, creamy white to ivory, and dotted red to purple. The column is short, stout, and incurved.

Cultivation

Cymbidium canaliculatum requires warm growing conditions (summer daytime 77°F/25°C, nighttime 68°F/20°C, lower in winter) and can stand both full sunshine and shade. A humid atmosphere and good air movement are required, and it should be potted in a free-draining medium.

Classification

Cymbidium canaliculatum R. Brown 1810.

Cymbidium canaliculatum

Cymbidium dayanum

This evergreen orchid occurs widely in Asia, in northeast India, southeast China, Taiwan, Japan, Indochina, Sumatra, Borneo, and the Philippines. *Cymbidium dayanum* is an epiphyte, often found on rotten logs and tree stumps, growing at elevations of more than 6,700 feet (2,000 m).

It has strongly compressed to ellipsoid pseudobulbs. The leaves are gracefully arching, acute, narrow, thick-textured, and up to 4 feet (1.2 m) long. The arching inflorescence is up to 14 inches (35 cm) long. The flowers are fragrant with unequal, oblong to lanceolate sepals and petals that are creamy to white in color. They have a central streak or stripe of maroon running toward the apex and a maroon border. There are two ridges on the callus, with forward-pointing, erect lateral lobes. The lip is white, marked with maroon and an orangey red base.

Cultivation

Pot *Cymbidium dayanum* in a free-draining compost of coarse bark or coarse peat substitute mix. Apply copious water in the summer, and periodically feed one-quarter strength fertilizer. Place in a bright but shaded position. It is best grown all year round in warm temperatures (summer day 77°F/25°C, night 68°F/20°C), but it can tolerate cooler conditions. It does not need a rest period in the winter.

Classification

Cymbidium dayanum Reichenbach f. 1869.

This dark wine-colored form of *Cymbidium dayanum* from Borneo was originally described as a separate species, *C. angustifolium*.

Cymbidium devonianum

This epiphytic orchid grows in mountainous areas of Nepal, northeast India (Sikkim, Meghalaya), Bhutan, and northern Thailand, at altitudes from 4,750 to 7,200 feet (1,450–2,200 m). This species is of considerable ornamental and horticultural importance, since it has been used widely in hybridizing and can be found in the background of many late-flowering miniature and intermediate cymbidiums.

It has small ovoid pseudobulbs bearing two or more thick, leathery, and grooved leaves. The inflorescence is a pendulous raceme, 6 to 17 inches (15–43 cm) long, producing between 15 and 35 closely spaced flowers. The flowers are olive green, spotted red to brown with purple streaks, and the petals are a little shorter than the sepals. The reddish purple lip is three-lobed. The column is greenish yellow, spotted red at its apex, with two small wings toward the apex.

Cultivation

Cymbidium devonianum prefers cool to intermediate temperatures (61°F/16°C to 68°F/20°C in the day, 55°F/13°C to 64°F/18°C at night, lower in winter). This cloud-forest plant requires well-drained but water-retentive compost, which must not be allowed to dry out during the growth period. A short rest period is recommended in winter.

Classification

Cymbidium devonianum Paxton 1843.

Cymbidium devonianum

Cymbidium lowianum

This is an epiphytic or lithophytic orchid native to southwest China, Myanmar (Burma), and Thailand. It has compressed pseudobulbs with leaf bases in two rows. Leaves are 20 to 36 inches (50–91 cm) long and pointed at the apex. The inflorescence is an arching raceme, up to 5.2 feet (160 cm) long, bearing 15 to 26 flowers up to 4 inches (10 cm) across. The sepals and petals are yellowish green and veined brownish red to red. The sepals are vaguely keeled behind the petals. The lip is yellow; the side lobes are a subdued yellow, and the midlobe is white at the base and has a bold V-shaped patch of maroon to purple (sometimes yellow or orange). The column is spotted red with a yellow base.

There are three distinct forms in which the V-shaped mark on the lip varies in color. In *Cymbidium lowianum* var. *lowianum* it is maroon to purple, in *C. l.* var. *concolor* it is yellow, and in *C. l.* var. *i'ansonii* it is orange.

Cultivation

Pot in open well-drained compost comprising coarse bark with a water-retentive additive such as sphagnum moss. Grow in cool to intermediate temperatures (61–68°F/16–20°C during the day, 55–64°F/13–18°C at night, lower in winter), with bright but shaded light. These orchids can be placed outside during warm weather but should be brought indoors at the first sign of frost.

Classification

Cymbidium lowianum Reichenbach f. 1879.

Cymbidium lowianum

Cymbidium tigrinum

This miniature lithophytic orchid grows on bare rocks and in rock crevices in open situations. It is native to Myanmar (Burma) and northeast India, growing at altitudes of 4,900 to 8,860 feet (1,500–2,700 m). It grows to only about 8 inches (20 cm) tall.

It has ovoid to ovoid-conical pseudobulbs that have basal sheaths and bear three to five lanceolate and leathery leaves. The inflorescence is upright with a nodding tip, 6 to 8 inches (15–20 cm) long, bearing three to six flowers. The flowers are honey scented, 2 inches (5 cm) in diameter, with the sepals and petals a muted yellowish green, lightly veined, and spotted purple. The column is long, pale olive green, spotted with red. The oblong lip is three-lobed; the side lobes are erect, while the midlobe is oblong.

Cultivation

Since *Cymbidium tigrinum* is usually found growing on rocky mountains and in crevices it needs a good compost of coarse bark and sphagnum moss, with added gritty sand to make a porous mix. Good but shaded light, high humidity, and excellent air movement are other requirements. It is a cool-growing plant that requires temperatures in the following range: summer daytime 61°F (16°C), nighttime 55°F (13°C); winter daytime 55°F (13°C), nighttime 50°F (10°C).

Classification

Cymbidium tigrinum Parish ex Hooker 1864.

Cymbidium tigrinum

Cymbidium tracyanum

Perhaps the most spectacular and fragrant of all the species in the genus, *Cymbidium tracyanum* is found in Myanmar (Burma), Thailand, and China. It is either an epiphyte growing on trees, its distinctive arching inflorescence cascading down, or a lithophyte growing on damp rocks in damp shaded forest, often near or overhanging streams. In cultivation it has been used extensively in hybridizing because it produces large specimen plants and it has a strong scent.

The pseudobulbs are compressed and are covered with two rows of leaf bases. The leaves are linear to ligulate, up to 38 inches (96 cm), and positively keeled beneath. The inflorescence is longer than the leaves at 4.3 feet (1.3 m), and bears up to 20 flowers. The flowers are up to 5 inches (13 cm) across; the sepals and petals are greenish yellow and distinctively marked with brown to reddish stripes. The petals are narrowly oblong. The lip is three-lobed, creamy yellow spotted with red; the side lobes are roundish and erect.

Cultivation

Cymbidium tracyanum needs an open compost, with plenty of water and feed during the growing period. During the winter rest period, however, only sufficient water should be given to keep the pseudobulbs plump. Good but shaded light, high humidity ,and excellent air movement are other requirements. This cool-growing plant prefers temperatures in the following range: summer daytime 61°F (16°C), nighttime 55°F (13°C); winter daytime 55°F (13°C), nighttime 50°F (10°C).

Classification

Cymbidium tracyanum L. Castle 1890.

Cymbidium tracyanum

Other *Cymbidium* Species

Cymbidium ensifolium from tropical and temperate East Asia.

Cymbidium longifolium from northeast India, Nepal, Myanmar (Burma), and southwest China.

Cymbidium chloranthum from Malesia.

171

Cymbidium Hybrids

Cymbidium Evening Star 'Cooksbridge'

Cymbidium 'Plush Canyon'

Cymbidium 'Sayonar

Cymbidium Sutherland 'Cooksbridge'

Cymbidium lowianum 'Long Spray'

Cynorkis

DATA

Number of Species: About 125.

Classification: *Cynorkis* Thouars 1809; tribe Orchideae, subtribe Habenariinae.

Form: Mostly terrestrial orchids, a few lithophytes and epiphytes, with tuberous, fleshy roots. The stems are often glandular and hairy. Leaves are sparse sheathing the stems. The inflorescence is a terminal raceme bearing one to many flowers. The flowers are long lasting, pink, mauve, or purple (sometimes with white or orange), produced in loose or dense clusters. The dorsal sepal, along with the petals, forms a hood. The lip is entire or lobed, usually larger in size than the sepals, and with a spur.

Distribution: Africa, Madagascar, Mascarene Islands.

Habitat: Dry rocky areas, mossy riverbank edges, on tree trunks, forested areas, grasslands, from sea level to 5,500 ft (1,700 m).

The name for the genus derives from the Greek *kynos* ("dog") and *orchis* ("testicles"), referring to the testicle-shaped tuberous fleshy roots. The genus is closely allied to *Habenaria*, differing in flower structure. Nearly all the species are native to Madagascar, with about 20 species on mainland Africa. They are deciduous species, shedding their leaves in the winter. Mature plants are self-pollinating and readily set seed, which germinates easily under warm, humid conditions.

Cultivation

Members of this genus should be grown under similar conditions to *Disa*. Provide a rich porous compost that will be water retentive during the vital growing season but that will become dryer once the tubers go into their rest and maturation period. While resting, they must have sufficient moisture to stop desiccation of the tubers. Grow in clay pots with tubers sunk into fresh moss, with pieces of broken pot in the base. Give shaded light once new growth is seen. When growth appears, water the plant carefully, increasing the amount given as it grows. Start off in the greenhouse and place the pot outside on warm days. Keep only just moist as the plant dies back and provide cool conditions throughout the winter rest period.

Once all signs of green have gone, the tubers may be taken carefully from the pot and divided before being repotted. Keep newly potted tubers just moist until the next year's new growth appears.

The temperature range required depends on the native region, habitat, and altitude of each species.

Cynorkis purpurascens 'Saint Germain's Blessing'; in the wild this species comes from the Mascarenes and Madagascar.

Cypripedium

DATA

Number of Species: About 45.

Classification: *Cypripedium* Linnaeus 1753; tribe Cypripedieae, subtribe Cypripediinae.

Form: Terrestrial orchids, less than 39 in (100 cm) tall, with a stout creeping rhizome and fleshy roots. Stem short to long, slender, sheathed, bearing one to four plicate, ribbed leaves. Showy single to several flowers are borne on a raceme and are variously colored. Dorsal sepals are erect, ovate to elliptical; lateral sepals are united most of length, point downward, and are held behind the lip. Petals are narrow, spreading, and twisted, smaller than sepals. Lip is inflated and pouch-shaped with top margins rolled inward. The column is short and bears a pair of fertile stamens on its sides.

Distribution: Europe, Asia to China and Japan, Mexico, North America.

Habitat: Swamps, bogs, wooded slopes, scrub.

The most distinctive feature of this group of orchids is the inflated pouchlike lip that resembles a slipper, hence the common names of slipper orchids, lady's slippers, and mocassin flowers that are variously applied to these species. The scientific name *Cypripedium* is derived from the name of the Greek island of Cyprus (*cypros*), which was sacred to Venus, and the word *pedilon* (corrupted to *pedium*), meaning "slipper." The pouch encloses the reproductive organs. In this genus there is a third stamen which is sterile and forms a large petalloid staminode.

Throughout the world these orchids have been heavily collected in the past and virtually wiped out in many parts, such as the British Isles. In many places it is now illegal to collect them from the wild, so it is critical to ensure that any specimens marketed are from reputable commercial outlets and bred in cultivation through plant division or from seed raised from cultivated plants.

Cultivation

Compost and growing conditions are very variable and will depend entirely on the individual species. In their natural habitat, species of this genus may be found on acid or alkaline soils, in full sun, shade, or dappled shade. Most suitable mixes can be made up from the following: limestone, peat substitute, leaf mold, coarse grit or sand. Sphagnum moss and loam can be added. Give evenly moist conditions. Once the leaves have died down, give less water and give a leaf-mold top dressing in winter while the plant is at rest. If the plant is more suited to boggy conditions, prepare the ground in advance.

Cypripedium fargesii occurs in China, where it is Critically Endangered.

Cypripedium calceolus

Occurring throughout Europe, temperate Asia, and North America, this species of orchid is the most widespread of the genus. It inhabits shaded forests with lime-rich soil from sea level to 8,300 feet (2,500 m). The two subspecies occurring in North America (*Cypripedium calceolus pubescens* and *C. c. parviflorum*) are sometimes regarded as distinct species—*C. pubescens* (Large Yellow Lady's Slipper, or American Valerian) and *C. parviflorum* (Lesser Yellow Lady's Slipper)— or sometimes both are deemed to be subspecies of *C. parviflorum*.

Cypripedium calceolus is an erect terrestrial herb up to 32 inches (81 cm) tall, arising from a creeping rhizome. There are three or four elliptical to ovate leaves, 2 to 8 inches (5–20 cm) long, sheathing at the base. The inflorescence is erect, with one or two flowers. The flowers are showy, large, and have dark maroon sepals and petals. The dorsal sepal is twisted, ovate to lanceolate, while the lateral sepals are joined at the apex. The pouchlike lip is yellow with red spots on the inside and with incurved pouch margins.

Cultivation

Because *C. calceolus* is a protected species you should only grow plants that have come from a legal source. In any case, transplanted plants rarely succeed. If the new plant is in a large enough pot, then follow instructions given at the time of purchase. If the plant is to be grown in a garden situation, it will require moist alkaline soil (add limestone) and a mid-shade outlook. Protect it from frost during the winter months and give a mulch of leaf mold. Always ensure good drainage but keep surrounding soils moist.

Classification

Cypripedium calceolus Linnaeus 1753.

Cypripedium calceolus

Cypripedium reginae

The Pink-and-White Lady's Slipper, or Showy Lady's Slipper (*Cypripedium reginae*), occurs in eastern North America, mostly at lower altitudes up to 2,000 feet (600 m) in damp woods, bogs, swamps, fen meadows, and similar moist habitats, where it flowers from May to August. Like all cypripediums, it is a protected species and is the state flower of Minnesota. Not only is illegal collection of this plant a cause for concern, the species is also threatened by habitat destruction, including wetland drainage.

It grows up to 36 inches (91 cm), with three to seven leaves arising from a stout rhizome. The leaves are ovate to lanceolate, 4 to 10 inches (10–25 cm) in length. The inflorescence is erect and bears up to three flowers. The sepals and petals are white; the lip is pink, streaked with white. The dorsal sepals are obtuse or rounded, while the lateral sepals are fused. The petals are spreading, oblong to oblong-elliptical. The lip is inflated, with infolded margins. The staminode is yellow and white with red spotting.

Cultivation

A compost mix comprising coarse grit or sand, leaf mold, and loam is required. If a garden position is envisaged, it is best to prepare the site thoroughly before obtaining the specimen. A shady cool position is best. This species benefits from two to three hours' direct sunlight in the early morning or late afternoon and dappled shade for the remainder of the day. It forms good clumps in the right conditions.

Classification

Cypripedium reginae Walter 1788.

Cypripedium reginae

Dendrobium

DATA

Number of Species: Over 1,200.

Classification: *Dendrobium* Swartz 1709; tribe Dendrobieae, subtribe Dendrobiinae.

Form: Very large, variable genus. Canelike or fleshy, erect or creeping pseudobulbs from 0.4 in (1 cm) long to stemlike. One to many leaves. Racemose inflorescence may be erect, pendent, or horizontal, bearing one to many showy flowers. Petals are narrow, broader than sepals on occasions. The lip is entire or three-lobed. Column is short, terete or subterete; foot of column is joined to lip and lateral sepals. There are four pollinia in two pairs without caudicles or a stipe.

Distribution: India, Southeast Asia, China, Malaysia, Australia, Philippines, New Guinea, New Zealand, Pacific Islands.

Habitat: Very variable from cool to warm, sun to shade, lowlands to highlands. Epiphytic or lithophytic, rarely terrestrial.

Because of the large number of species in the genus, dendrobiums vary considerably in size, color, and growing conditions—the last a reflection of the variety of habitats and altitudes in which they grow. They are found in hot jungles, in mountains as high as 10,000 feet (3,000 m), in swamps, semiarid regions, and much in between. The classification of the genus is under constant review and it is likely that in the future many will be reallocated to other genera and renamed. The number of species is more than matched by the quantity of hybrids that have been and continue to be developed. In addition to appearing as pot plants, dendrobiums are well represented in the cut-flower trade.

Cultivation

With the immense range of species and hybrids available, follow closely the individual cultural instructions given by the grower. Depending on the species these orchids can be planted in pots, pans, or baskets, or even tied to cork bark blocks. Suitable growing media can be coconut chunks or husks, coarse peat substitute, coarse to medium bark, perlite, charcoal, perlag, or a mix of any of these. Whatever medium is used it must be free-draining since dendrobiums do not like to have their "feet wet." Keep the plants frost-free, water well while growing, and feed every two to four weeks. Withdraw water when they are resting, maintaining just enough moisture to prevent the canes and pseudobulbs from shriveling. Keep the humidity high, with a good flow of air, and give maximum light in the fall. If a lot of small keikis (young plants) appear, this indicates that the plants are receiving too much warmth and water.

Dendrobium densiflorum occurs from the Himalayas east to China.

Dendrobium brymerianum

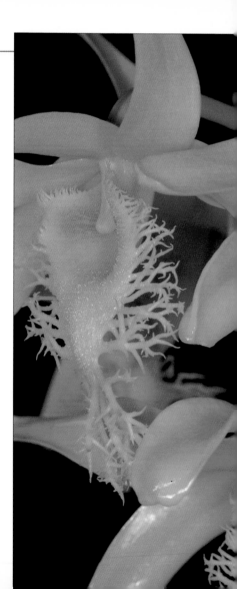

This orchid grows at 4,750 to 5,250 feet (1,450–1,600 m) in northeastern India, northern Thailand, Myanmar (Burma), northern Laos, and southwestern China. Its stems are swollen in the middle and terete in shape, bearing up to six leaves which are 2 to 5 inches (5–13 cm) long, leathery and acute, with the upper surface grooved. The racemose inflorescence arises near the apex of mature pseudobulbs and is 4 to 16 inches (10–40 cm) long, producing one to three fragrant yellow flowers, 2 to 2.5 inches (5–6 cm) across. The sepals and petals are twisted slightly. The lip is large, with distinct threads around the margin.

Cultivation

An open medium, plenty of air movement, an intermediate temperature range, and good light should be provided. Water well and feed every two to four weeks while growing. Allow to dry out a little over the winter. Repot every two to three years or if the medium breaks down. This species does not like stale compost or "wet feet."

Classification

Dendrobium brymerianum Reichenbach f. 1875.

Dendrobium brymerianum

Dendrobium kingianum

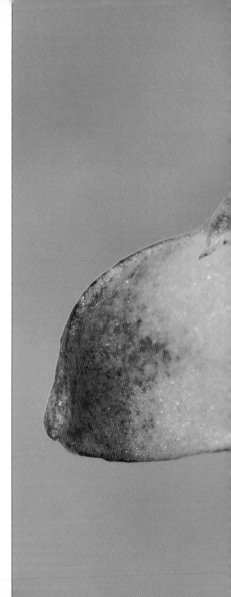

This highly variable lithophytic, clump-forming orchid occurs in the eastern half of Australia at 165 to 4,000 feet (50–1,200 m), on the coast and in the mountains. Although variable in form, it can be grown in a range of situations. It has also been widely used in hybridization.

The stems are slightly plump at the base, erect, and up to 24 inches (60 cm) in length, bearing two to seven leaves. The leaves are ovate or obovate. The inflorescence is usually erect, bearing up to 16 white through pink to dark mauve, fragrant flowers. The three-lobed lip is sometimes striped a darker color. The midlobe is recurved and acute, with a fleshy callus.

Cultivation

It can be grown in pots or shallow containers using an open medium or on cork bark, with its roots wrapped in sphagnum moss. Provide plenty of water when in growth, bright light (but not direct sun), good air circulation, and a humid atmosphere. Reduce water during the dormant period from mid-fall through spring.

Classification

Dendrobium kingianum Bidwill 1844.

Dendrobium kingianum

Dendrobium speciosum

This highly variable species is found in southeast Australia from the coastline to about 150 miles (240 km) inland. It grows as a lithophyte on rocks at the base of cliffs or in open forests, and to the north of its range as an epiphyte in rain forests high up in the trees, where the air circulation is excellent.

The pseudobulbous stems are 3 to 39 inches (8–100 cm) long, cylindrical, swollen at the base, and bear two to five leaves at the apex. The leaves are leathery, oblong, and 10 inches (25 cm) long. The inflorescence can be erect or pendent. It is 24 inches (60 cm) in length and is densely covered in many very fragrant, white, whitish cream, or yellow flowers. The flowers open in the daytime and close on cooler evenings. The sepals and petals are striped with purple, brown, or red and are linear to lanceolate in shape. The three-lobed lip is white with yellow at the base. The lateral lobes are erect and marked red or purple.

Cultivation

Because of the climatic differences between the northern and southern parts of this species' natural habitat, temperature requirements vary when it is grown in cultivation. It is therefore important to try to determine where plant originated. Northern types generally require warm conditions and a rest period, during which time bright light is needed to help induce flowering. Southern types usually need cool conditions. Grow in an open medium with plenty of fresh air and air movement. Water well while the plants are in growth.

Classification

Dendrobium speciosum J. E. Smith 1805.

Dendrobium speciosum

Other *Dendrobium* Species

Dendrobium hellwigianum from New Guinea.

Dendrobium lawesii from New Guinea to the Solomon Islands.

Dendrobium unicum from Indochina.

Overleaf (pages 196-97): *Dendrobium bracteosum* from the Moluccas to the Bismarck Archipelago.

Dendrobium vexillarius, also from the Moluccas to the Bismarck Archipelago.

Dendrobium finisterrae from New Guinea.

Dendrobium tobaense from Sumatra.

198

Dendrobium secundum from Indochina to west and central Malesia.

Dendrobium Hybrids

Dendrobium 'New Guinea'

Dendrobium Pink Beauty 'Queen'

Dendrochilum

DATA

Number of Species: About 150.

Classification: *Dendrochilum*
Blume 1825; tribe Coelogyneae,
subtribe Coelogyninae.

Form: Creeping rhizome with ovoid
to cylindrical pseudobulbs well
spaced or clustered along length.
Pseudobulbs sheathed by papery
bracts; bear one or two leaves at
the apex. Leaves tough, oblong
to lanceolate, acute, and rolled
up in the bud. Inflorescence is a
slender spike or raceme, suberect
to pendulous, densely covered in
thin-textured fragrant flowers
arranged in two ranks. Sepals are
fused to base of column and are
larger than petals. Lip is oblong,
erect, and spreading. Column is
winged at the tip; there are four
waxy pollinia.

Distribution: Southeast Asia,
Indonesia, Philippines, New
Guinea.

Habitat: Epiphytic and lithophytic
in mountains and forested areas.

These are small to medium plants with dense clusters of pseudobulbs.
Their genus name is derived from the Greek *dendron* ("tree") and
cheilo ("lip"), an allusion to the prominence of the lip. They are popularly
known as golden chain orchids because of their arching and pendent
clusters of fragrant yellowish flowers. The genus is allied to *Pholidota*
and *Coelogyne*.

Cultivation

These orchids like to be pot-bound and will not tolerate disturbance
of their roots. They will form elegant clumps. Dendrochilums can be
grown in sphagnum moss and bound tightly to a bark or tree-fern block.
They need plenty of water during active growth and, while they do not
have a true rest period, growth does slow down. Reduce the amount
of water at this time, giving just enough to keep the medium moist.
Provide cool to intermediate temperatures with bright shaded light
and plenty of air movement.

Dendrochilum lewisii is from Mount Mulu, Sarawak.

Dendrochilum cobbianum

In its natural habitat *Dendrochilum cobbianum* can be found growing in full sun on rocks or clinging to tree trunks or branches. This showy orchid from the Philippines will stand out. It has narrow, conical, clustered pseudobulbs with a single apical leaf. The inflorescence is longer than the leaf and droops some 12 inches (30 cm) in total length. Its flowers, with their dull white petals and sepals and yellow to orange lip, make for a glorious sight.

Cultivation

This orchid likes to be pot-bound and does not tolerate disturbance of its roots. It can be grown in sphagnum moss and bound tightly to a bark or tree-fern block. It needs plenty of water during active growth and, although it does not have a true rest period, growth does slow down. Reduce the amount of water at this time, giving just enough to keep the medium moist. Provide cool to intermediate temperatures with bright shaded light and plenty of air movement.

Classification

Dendrochilum cobbianum Reichenbach f. 1880.

Dendrochilum cobbianum

Dendrochilum glumaceum

This epiphytic orchid is found growing on trees and rocks up to 6,000 feet (1,800 m) in the Philippines. The arching inflorescence admirably displays the clusters of flowers. The pseudobulbs are ovoid and clustered with a single leaf at the tip. The leaf is up to 18 inches (45 cm) long, erect, and grasslike in appearance. The inflorescence is up to 20 inches (50 cm) long and bears many white flowers, which have a bright orange to yellow lip.

Cultivation

This orchid likes to be pot-bound and does not tolerate disturbance of its roots. It can be grown in sphagnum moss and bound tightly to a bark or tree-fern block. It needs plenty of water during active growth and, although it does not have a true rest period, growth does slow down. Reduce the amount of water at this time, giving just enough to keep the medium moist. Provide cool to intermediate temperatures with bright shaded light and plenty of air movement.

Classification

Dendrochilum glumaceum Lindley 1878.

Dendrochilum glumaceum

206

Dimorphorchis

DATA

Number of Species: About 3.

Classification: *Dimorphorchis*
Rolfe 1919; tribe Vandeae,
subtribe Sarcanthinae.

Form: Orchids often with
branching stems, which are
erect or arched, up to 6.6 ft
(2 m) long. The leaves are
distichous, ligulate, leathery,
sheathed near base, and 28
to 36 in (70–90 cm) long. The
inflorescence is pendent and
loosely covered with many
flowers. The flowers are large,
often fragrant (more so with
basal flowers) and come in
two forms (dimorphic), with
variations in color, size,
fragrance, and other features.
Sepals and petals nearly similar,
linear to oblong. The lip is fleshy,
saccate, three-lobed, with the
midlobe raised as a median keel.
Column is short and fleshy. There
are four pollinia in two pairs.

Distribution: Endemic to Borneo.

Habitat: Epiphytic on trees in
riverside and montane forests.

The most significant feature of these orchids, which are similar to
Vanda species, to which they are related, is the dimorphic nature of
the flowers. For example, in *Dimorphorchis rossii* the upper flowers are
orange and fragrant while the lower flowers are yellow and not fragrant.
Similarly, in *D. lowii* the lower flowers are strongly fragrant and yellow
with purple spots. By contrast, the apical flowers are less yellow, they
have large maroon blotches, they are not fragrant, and they are larger
than the lower flowers. In fact, the name *Dimorphorchis* is derived from
the Greek *di* ("two") and *morphe* ("shape"), alluding to the differing
flower forms that can occur on the inflorescence.

Cultivation

Growing conditions are similar to those of *Vanda* species—consistent
temperature and humidity are important, and seasonal variations are
to be avoided. *Dimorphorchis* species require high humidity, continuous
watering, good air circulation, and dappled shade. Larger plants require
staking to support the leaves and the pendent inflorescence. Small
plants can be grown in baskets with a mix of very free-draining media.

Dimorphorchis rossii (lower flower) is a native of northern Borneo.

Diplocaulobium

DATA

Number of Species: About 100.

Classification: *Diplocaulobium*
Reichenbach f. Kranzun 1910;
tribe Epidendreae, subtribe
Dendrobiinae.

Form: Small to medium epiphytes
with one-leaved pseudobulbs
on a creeping rhizome. The
pseudobulbs are swollen at the
base and tapered toward the
apex. The solitary leaves are
apical, erect, or suberect. The
inflorescence is sessile and single
flowered. Flowers vary from dull
to showy, and from small to
medium in size. The lip is entire
to three–lobed. There are four
pollinia in close pairs.

Distribution: Malaysia, Australia,
Pacific Islands, New Guinea.

Habitat: Grows in full sun or
dappled sun in forests up to
4,500 ft (1,500 m).

The creeping stem and swollen pseudobulbs are alluded to in the name of the genus, which comes from the Greek words *diplous* ("folded," or "double"), *caulos* ("stem"), and lobion ("lobe").

Diplocaulobium species are ephemeral flowering plants, meaning that the flowers last from just a few hours to less than a day. Most species come from New Guinea. Flower color includes white, cream, yellowish, and greenish to shades of red.

Cultivation

While their star-shaped flowers are attractive, these orchids are not often cultivated because of their ephemeral nature. In cultivation they should be grown on bark in good, slightly shaded light. Water well, but reduce the amount of water given when growth is complete. They can be propagated by division of the closely spaced pseudobulbs. Grow at intermediate greenhouse conditions and mist frequently.

Diplocaulobium arachnoideum is endemic to
New Guinea, where it grows in wet, humid forests.

Disa

DATA

Number of Species: About 130.

Classification: *Disa* Berg 1767; tribe Diseae, subtribe Disinae.

Form: Terrestrial herbs with ellipsoid tubers. The leaves are produced along the flowering stem or on separate sterile shoots. The inflorescence bears one to many flowers. The flowers are showy and come in various colors. The sepals are free; the dorsal sepal is erect forming a spur and hood. The petals are smaller, often lying inside the hood. The lip is small, narrow, and not spurred. The column is short with two pollinia, each with a caudicle and naked viscidium.

Distribution: South Africa, tropical Africa, Madagascar, and Mascarene Islands.

Habitat: Wet sides of streams on mountainsides where water is continually percolating beneath; also in rock crevices (where water has collected) and sandy well-drained, rich riverbeds.

The name *Disa* refers to Queen Disa in Swedish mythology. *Disa uniflora* (Berg) is probably one of the most cultivated species of the genus. *Disa* species are regarded by some as difficult to grow, but under the right conditions they make a beautiful display.

Disa veitchii was the first hybrid orchid to be bred. This was achieved by Veitch in 1891 by crossing *D. racemosa* with *D. uniflora*. Crossing of plants in this way to get bigger flowers, petals, or spikes is well known. Intercrossing of some *Disa* species has produced plants with inflorescences up to 39 inches (99 cm) long, bearing about 10 flowers.

Cultivation

Because these plants come from areas where water is always running over the roots, water is absolutely essential when cultivating them. A good open-drained compost is a must. Coarse river sand is ideal, with added sphagnum moss. An ebb and flow system, in which the pots are stood in a tray that is filled twice daily and allowed to filter back into the water reservoir, is a good method of watering. Roots must be kept moist while growing. Humidity must be maintained at 50 percent or higher; good air circulation and dappled shade should also be provided. Mist on hot days. Feed carefully with very weak balanced fertilizer. Dissolved salts should be no more than 200 ppm. Keep moist when the plants are at rest after flowering and the leaves have died back. Start minimal watering when new growth is seen, then increase as the plants grow. Propagate by division of new tubers or from the small tubers (stolons) that grow around the plant.

Disa x kewensis is a hybrid of D. uniflora and D. tripetaloides.

Disa uniflora

This terrestrial plant is renowned for its fragrant, long-lasting, strikingly red flowers. It occurs near fast-flowing streams, in rock crevices, and other wet areas on Table Mountain, South Africa. The stem is 6 to 28 inches (15–70 cm) long. The leaves are lanceolate with an acute tip and are borne up the stem, those close to the base being larger. The inflorescence bears one to three flowers, which are mainly brilliant scarlet red with orange to yellow on the petals. The sepals are broadly ovate with the dorsal sepal forming a hood, which has orange coloration inside. The petals are obovate or obovate to oblong. The lip is projecting with a recurved tip.

Cultivation

A good open-drained compost is a must. It should never be allowed to dry out. Coarse river sand is ideal, with added peat substitute or sphagnum moss. An ebb and flow system, in which the pots are stood in a tray that is filled twice daily and allowed to filter back into the water reservoir, is a good method of watering. Roots must be kept moist while growing. Humidity should be maintained at 50 percent or more; good air circulation and dappled shade should also be provided. Mist on hot days. Feed carefully with very weak balanced fertilizer. Dissolved salts should be no more than 200 ppm. Keep moist when the plants are at rest after flowering and the leaves have died back. Start minimal watering when new growth is seen, then increase the amount given as the plants grow.

Classification

Disa uniflora P. J. Bergius 1767.

Disa uniflora

Dockrillia

DATA

Number of Species: About 30.

Classification: *Dockrillia* Breiger 1981; tribe Dendrobieae, subtribe Dendrobiinae.

Form: Lacking pseudobulbs but with thin wiry stems and long fleshy cylindrical leaves that in most species trail from the trunks of trees. In others the leaves may be short and pencil-like or even greatly swollen and covered in warty bumps. The flowers grow in clusters and often appear scruffy owing to the long slender tepals, which may be twisted or curved in various directions. Most are pale. The lip may be ruffled and strongly recurved and is often marked with bright colors.

Distribution: Australia and the islands of Australasia from New Guinea to New Caledonia and Vanuatu, with the greatest diversity in tropical Queensland.

Habitat: Mainly epiphytic or lithophytic in tropical rain forest or more open forests at low to moderate altitudes.

Formerly listed within the large genus *Dendrobium*, the genus *Dockrillia* was recognized in 1981 to accommodate all species with fleshy cylindrical or terete leaves. It was named for the celebrated Australian amateur orchidologist Alick W. Dockrill—one of relatively few living botanists to be honored in this way. Some *Dockrillia* species appear to hybridize readily in the wild, and many cultivated hybrids have been developed.

Cultivation

Mature *Dockrillia* species are usually relatively easy to propagate by splitting the rhizome clusters. The temperate species are hardy and easy to grow both indoors and outside, but should be protected from frost. Most can be planted in small pots to create dense symmetrical displays, but slab media are usually used in order that the species can adopt their rather rambling natural habit. They usually require good air movement and year-round watering—but slightly less in winter.

A coastal inhabitant of central eastern Australia, *Dockrillia linguiforme (Dendrobium linguiforme)* forms large colonies on rocks or trees.

Dockrillia striolata

This species is named for its small fragrant drooping flowers, which bear delicately striped petals and sepals and a ruffled white lip. *Dockrillia striolata* is native to temperate southeastern Australia, including New South Wales, Victoria, and Tasmania. It is a popular species for cultivating in these areas and increasingly so in temperate climates elsewhere in the world. It is one of a group of *Dockrillia* species known in Australia as rock orchids—in the wild it normally grows in exposed locations as a lithophyte in cracks and crevices on cliff faces or between boulders. It flowers in late summer and fall.

It is also known by the name *Dendrobium striolatum*.

Cultivation

This attractive species is relatively easy to grow in cool to intermediate conditions, and it tolerates very cool nighttime temperatures. It can be grown outside in rock crevices or on trees, and indoors on slab media or in small baskets. Freshly divided clumps should be started off in fresh sphagnum moss, but the wiry roots will soon spread out over available surfaces. Indoor specimens should be watered and fed with dilute balanced fertilizer throughout the spring, summer, and fall, but both watering and feeding may be reduced in the winter months. The plants do best in bright light or partial shade.

Classification

Dockrillia striolata (Reichenbach f.) Rauschert 1983.

Dockrillia striolata

Dracula

DATA

Number of Species: About 100.

Classification: *Dracula* Luer 1978;
tribe Epidendreae, subtribe
Pleurothallidinae.

Form: Pseudobulbs are absent;
leaves grow from short densely
clustered stems. The long narrow
fleshy leaves have a distinct
midrib. The large, usually brightly
colored flowers appear on shoots
off the leaf stem and hang below
the plant. The large sepals taper
to very long narrow tails but the
petals are very small and sit
either side of the thick column,
giving the appearance of eyes
next to a prominent nose. There
are two pollinia. The lip takes on
a wide variety of elaborate forms
in different species.

Distribution: Central America and
northern South America from
southern Mexico to Peru; the
greatest diversity of species
occurs in Colombia and Ecuador.

Habitat: Mainly epiphytic,
occasionally terrestrial in
wet tropical forests.

Members of this dramatic group have been popular with European growers since the late 19th century, but at that time they were classified within the larger pleurothallid genus *Masdevallia*. The genus *Dracula* was formed in 1978 to accommodate species with hairy or warty flowers and a characteristic lip. The name is from the Greek meaning "little dragon," but in some species the heavily pigmented dark red, purple, or black flowers with their long pointed tails inevitably conjure up other, more sinister, interpretations of the name.

Cultivation

Dracula orchids are popular with growers but require patience and attention to detail to cultivate successfully. They do well growing in hanging baskets rooted in sphagnum moss and fir-bark compost. Open mesh baskets allow the flowers to emerge and hang from the base of the leaves. They should be protected from frosts in cool, shady greenhouse conditions. High humidity with good air movement is essential, and in dry weather the plants require daily misting as well as watering.

The striking 8-inch (20-cm) flowers give *Dracula vampira* a batlike appearance. This epiphytic species comes from Ecuador, where it is found at elevations of 6,000 to 7,200 feet (1,800–2,200 m).

Dracula berthae

The specimen of this orchid that was first recognized as a new species was found growing in the private collection of Colombian orchid enthusiast Bertha de Lasema of Bogotá, for whom it is named. In the wild, the species is known only from a small area of western Colombia at 7,500 to 8,500 feet (2,300-2,600 m) in the Andes. Bertha's Dracula, as it is commonly known, produces a single flower on each inflorescence. The sepals are fused and bear long tails, but the dorsal sepal—which is very dark purple, almost black—lacks a broad blade and is effectively all tail. The lateral sepals are white with dense dark purple to black speckles. The column and tiny petals are yellow. The lip is small and pale pink.

Cultivation

This species should be grown in cool to intermediate humid conditions with plenty of shade. It can be grown on a mossy slab or in a small basket loosely packed with moisture-retentive moss and open fibrous medium. It should be watered daily, ideally in the morning so that the leaves are dry by nightfall. Dilute fertilizer may be applied with the water once a week.

Classification

Dracula berthae Luer & Escobar 1979.

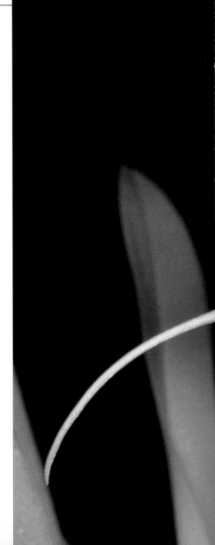

Dracula berthae

Other *Dracula* Species

Dracula cutis-bufonis from
northwestern Colombia.

Dracula trichroma from
Colombia and Ecuador.

Dracula robledorum
from Colombia.

Dryadella

DATA

Number of Species: About 40.

Classification: *Dryadella* Luer 1978; tribe Epidendreae, subtribe Pleurothallidinae.

Form: Small tuft-forming orchids with elongate fleshy leaves. Single-flowered inflorescences bloom in rapid succession, but their racemes are so short they are often hidden by the leaves. The flowers have short wide petals held at an angle to the lateral sepals, which bear distinctive calluses.

Distribution: Central America and northern South America from southern Mexico to southern Brazil.

Habitat: Epiphytes in low-lying temperate forests or at higher altitudes in the tropics.

These small and demure epiphytes are named for the wood nymphs of classical mythology but are less exotic in appearance than their name implies. The flowers bear green or yellowish tepals spotted with brown. By orchid standards they might even be considered drab, being small and often obscured by the leaves. As a result, they are relatively seldom cultivated. The group was previously considered part of the larger genus *Masdevallia*.

Cultivation

Most species can be grown successfully in small pots of well-drained epiphyte mix that mimic the restrictive nature of their natural habitat. They require regular watering all year round and prefer cool to intermediate temperatures.

Named for the tiny fictional kingdom of Lilliput in Jonathan Swift's fantasy novel *Gulliver's Travels*, *Dryadella lilliputiana* is widely distributed in southern Brazil at altitudes of 2,300 to 5,580 feet (700–1,700 m).

Dryadella edwallii

By far the most commonly cultivated member of its genus, *Dryadella edwallii* has the largest and most interesting flowers. Single specimens of this species are still rather unremarkable to look at, but a successfully cultivated cluster can form a striking display when in full bloom: a near spherical crown of fleshy leaves separated by the flowers, which are distinguished by long tails on the sepals.

The petals and sepals are pale green with purple spots. The lip is short and red and shaped like a human fingernail. *Dryadella edwallii* is named for the Swedish orchid collector G. Edwall. In the wild it grows mainly in Brazil.

Cultivation

These potentially large clusters can be grown in small pots or mounted on slabs. They require cool to intermediate temperatures and frequent watering and misting, but the roots must not become waterlogged, so good air movement around the plant is imperative—this can be achieved by hanging.

Classification

Dryadella edwallii (Cogniaux) Luer 1978.

Dryadella edwallii

Encyclia

DATA

Number of Species: About 150.

Classification: *Encyclia* Hooker 1828; tribe Epidendreae, subtribe Laeliinae.

Form: Fleshy leaves and dramatic flower spikes grow from the tip of thickened pseudobulbs. The inflorescences may be simple or branched but often form spectacular cascades. Individual flowers are small—less than 2 in (5 cm) across—but showy, with elongate, often colorful sepals and petals and an elaborate lip, the lateral lobes of which encircle the column (hence the genus name).

Distribution: From Florida through Central America and into tropical South America and islands of the West Indies.

Habitat: Mainly lithophytic or epiphytic on deciduous or coniferous trees in tropical woodlands with a pronounced winter dry season. Most species occur below a 3,300-ft (1,000-m) elevation.

This very popular group of orchids is renowned for its long-lasting and showy flowers, which produce dramatic displays *en masse* as well as being individually stunning. Members of the group were originally classified in the genus *Epidendrum*, which at the time included all epiphytic orchids. They were set aside in 1828, and by the late 20th century some 250 species were recognized in the genus. However, a molecular study in the mid-1990s resulted in about 100 species being carved off to form the new genera *Euchile*, *Prosthechea*, and *Dinema*. The change has caused some confusion and for commercial and horticultural purposes these new genera are still often regarded as part of the *Encyclia* group. One species, *E. citrina*, is one of rather few orchids with alleged medicinal properties—it was used by Native Americans in Central America to treat infected wounds.

Cultivation

Encyclia species grow well in pots or on slabs placed in dappled shade. Successful cultivation requires a tricky balance of copious watering without waterlogging in the growing season, followed by a rest period in which the medium but not the plant itself should dry out completely.

In Mexico *Prosthechea cochleata* (previously known as *Encyclia cochleata*) is referred to as *Pulpa*, meaning "octopus," because the lip resembles an octopus's body and its petals and sepals look like the tentacles. This rare plant grows as an epiphyte in swampy forests in parts of northern South America, Central America, and north into Florida.

Encyclia adenocaula

The epiphytic *Encyclia adenocaula* (*E. nemoralis*) grows on oak and pine trees from Mexico to Nicaragua, at altitudes between 1,500 and 6,000 feet (450–1,800 m). The leaves and inflorescences arise from the tip of stout egg-shaped pseudobulbs. In summer large clusters of pale pink flowers on long branching stems create cascading displays. With their long narrow petals and sepals, the flowers resemble spindly stars. The lip is in distinct sections—a pale pink and green hypochile and a flaring white epichile strongly marked with bright pink.

Cultivation

This tropical epiphyte does best mounted on a block of mossy bark. It requires intermediate temperatures but can tolerate being cool at night. By day it should be exposed to bright sunlight. It needs copious regular watering in the growing season only, and should be fed once a week with dilute balanced fertilizer. The plant should be allowed a rest from watering and feeding in winter, although regular light misting is beneficial. Without this rest it may fail to flower.

Classification

Encyclia adenocaula (Lallave and Lexarza) Schlechte 1918.

Encyclia adenocaula

Encyclia tampensis

This delightful species, known as the Butterfly Orchid, is a native of the Bahamas and Florida, where it is the most common wild orchid. It is epiphytic on living and dead trees and tolerates a wide range of growing conditions from the humidity of mangrove swamps to relatively exposed dry situations in open scrub.

The leaves are elongate and ovoid and sprout in threes from the tip of oval pseudobulbs. The flower spikes are simple or branching and the small 1.4-inch (3.5-cm) flowers are long-lasting and distinctive, with greenish brown petals and sepals and a broad white lip with a large bight pink spot. The plant does extremely well under cultivation and has been used to create numerous popular hybrids.

Cultivation
Easily cultivated outside from seed or propagated by division and requiring no further care in its native Florida, *Encyclia tampensis* can be grown under glass in temperate climates elsewhere. It can be planted in a pot or shallow pan in free-draining epiphyte compost or mounted on a bark slab. It tolerates a range of light conditions from full strong sunlight to partial shade. Regular watering, misting, and light feeding with a balanced fertilizer should be maintained throughout the growing season, with a rest in winter.

Classification
Encyclia tampensis (Lindley) Small 1913.

Encyclia tampensis

Epidendrum

DATA

Number of Species: About 1,000.

Classification: *Epidendrum*
Linnaeus 1763; tribe
Epidendreae, subtribe Laeliinae.

Form: Variable. Most species
have reedlike stems lacking
pseudobulbs, although
pseudobulbs are present in a
few. Flowers are borne in apical,
lateral, or basal inflorescences
that may be branched or simple.
The lip is fringed and fused to
the column for much of its
length. There are usually four,
occasionally two, pollinia.

Distribution: North, Central,
and South America from the
Carolinas to northern Argentina,
with the center of diversity in
equatorial South America.

Habitat: Very diverse—mainly
epiphytic or lithophytic in a
broad range of tropical and
subtropical habitats from sea
level to several thousand feet.

The genus *Epidendrum* was one of the first orchid genera to be
formally described, and the composition of the group has changed
considerably since it was established. The genus was named by the
Swedish father of taxonomy, Carolus Linnaeus, for the habit of many
of its members of growing in forks and crevices of tree trunks and
branches. The scientific name *Epidendrum* translates literally as "upon
a tree," and Linnaeus included in the group all the epiphytic orchids he
knew, many of which have since been reclassified. Not all members of
the group are exclusively epiphytic—there are lithophytic and terrestrial
examples, too. Given the diverse nature of the species in this group,
it is not surprising that many have ended up here, after having been
previously assigned to other genera.

Cultivation

Most cultivated *Epidendrum* species require intermediate conditions
of temperature and light, but other requirements vary considerably
according to species. Those species with reedlike stems may be grown
in beds, while those with pseudobulbs may be potted in free-draining
compost. All require regular watering during the growing season.

Epidendrum piliferum occurs in Costa Rica, Nicaragua, and Panama.

Epidendrum cristatum

This is a large, often terrestrial, sometimes epiphytic, orchid from tropical Central and South America. It has reed- or canelike stems up to 3 feet (90 cm) tall and an extensive root system. Each stem is sheathed at its base by long ovate to lanceolate leaves and gives rise to one or more terminal, fragrant, many-flowered inflorescences. The sepals and petals are pale yellowish green with red or brown spots. The lip is fused for much of its length to a stout column, while its free portion forms an elaborate lobed comb.

Cultivation

The plant should be grown in a large pot with free-draining epiphyte compost and placed in dappled sunlight or partial shade. It requires year-round warmth, watering, and feeding, reflecting its tropical distribution.

Classification

Epidendrum cristatum Ruiz Lopez & Pavón 1798.

Epidendrum cristatum

Epidendrum radioferens

A Central American native with a climbing canelike growth habit, *Epidendrum radioferens* produces clusters of pendent dark reddish brown flowers in winter. The stems are bound to support structures by clusters of rhizomes. Pseudobulbs are absent. The lip bears a frilly lower margin and three raised white markings radiating from its junction with the column, hence its scientific name, which means "ray-lipped" epidendrum.

Cultivation

This surprisingly hardy species can be grown outside in tropical, subtropical, or even warm temperate conditions but it needs to be protected from frost. It does well in a large pot and should be rooted in standard free-draining orchid compost and watered daily.

Classification

Epidendrum radioferens (Ames, F. T. Hubb & C. Schweinfurth) Hagsater 1977.

Epidendrum radioferens

Epidendrum stamfordianum

This strictly tropical species occurs naturally in low-lying areas of Central America and northern South America. It grows as an epiphyte on trees in open forests and is often found in plantations. Leathery leaves arise from 10-inch- (25-cm-) long pseudobulbs, while the dense branching inflorescences of spotty yellow and white, occasionally pink, flowers appear in winter from the basal rhizome. The flowers are just under 2 inches (5 cm) in diameter and last several weeks.

This plant was named for the English orchid enthusiast and patron of botanical science, Lord Stamford.

Cultivation

This elegant showy species requires patience to grow, since it responds to disturbance with a period of dormancy that may last a year or two. It is best grown mounted on a slab in a moderately warm, partially shaded spot. It should be watered and fed regularly with dilute balanced fertilizer and requires an annual period of rest—watering should be suspended in spring after flowering.

Classification:

Epidendrum stamfordianum Bateman 1839.

Epidendrum stamfordianum

Other *Epidendrum* Species

Epidendrum purum from western South America to Venezuela.

Epidendrum fragrans (Prosthechea fragrans) from tropical America.

Left: *Epidendrum mathewsii* from Ecuador and Peru.   Above: *Epidendrum mancum* from Ecuador to Peru.

Epidendrum difforme from
the Lesser Antilles.

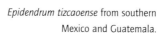

Epidendrum tizcaoense from southern
Mexico and Guatemala.

Epigeneium

DATA

Number of Species: About 35.

Classification: *Epigenium* Gagnepain 1932; tribe Dendrobieae, subtribe Dendrobiinae.

Form: Short pseudobulbs arise from long scrambling rhizomes. Each pseudobulb has two or three elongate leathery leaves with a pronounced midrib. The flowers bloom singly or on racemose inflorescences of a few to many large, long-lasting blooms. The sepals and petals are elongate and simple and may be white or intensely pigmented and patterned. The lip is three-lobed with a short mentum.

Distribution: South and East Asia from India and China to Indonesia and the Philippines.

Habitat: Most species are epiphytic scramblers high up on tall trees in wet tropical forests, at altitudes up to 8,000 ft (2,400 m).

The dramatic and long-lasting flowers of these upland Asian epiphytes make them popular with growers, but their rambling habit means they are not really suited to compact potted displays. Before being classified as a genus in their own right, these species were listed within *Dendrobium*, then by some authorities in *Katherinea*. If that was not confusing enough they are sometimes described as belonging to a fourth genus, *Sarcopodium*. It is likely the confusion will ultimately be resolved by molecular sequencing.

Cultivation

Epigeneium species are best grown in baskets or large shallow pans that give the rhizomes the opportunity to spread. A fibrous epiphyte compost mixed with charcoal is ideal, since it provides a very light, open, free-draining medium that will help keep the roots moist but not waterlogged. Regular light watering, high humidity, and good air movement are all important.

A hot- to cool-growing epiphyte, *Epigeneium chapaense* occurs on mossy branches of trees in humid forests in Vietnam.

Epigeneium stella-silvae

This striking native of Philippine rain forests is *Epigeneium stella-silvae* (*Dendrobium stella-silvae*). It has been known by at least four scientific names because, along with other related species, it has been bounced from genus to genus. The most recent change came in 1975, when it was placed in *Epigeneium* by the botanist Victor Summerhayes.

The plant itself is a robust rambling epiphyte with dark green leathery leaves. In the gloom of the forest the bright white flowers shine like clusters of five-pointed stars.

Cultivation

Like other members of its genus, *E. stella-silvae* grows best in an open medium, in a basket, or in a shallow pan. Alternatively, it can be mounted on a block of bark or tree fern. The plant needs year-round warmth and humidity. It will not tolerate stale or waterlogged compost around its root system, however, so good drainage and air movement are essential. Dilute feed should be watered in every few weeks.

Classification

Epigeneium stella-silvae (Loher & Kraenzle) Summerhayes 1957.

Epigeneium stella-silvae

252

Epipactis

DATA

Number of Species: About 35.

Classification: *Epipactis* Zinn 1757 (nom. cons.); tribe Neottieae, subtribe Limodorinae.

Form: Fleshy rhizomes give rise to leafy stems up to 40 in (100 cm) tall with a terminal inflorescence of a few to many pale or brightly colored flowers. The lip comprises a heart-shaped or triangular epichile and a large cup- or chalice-shaped hypochile. Some species have reduced chlorophyll and appear bluish purple.

Distribution: Temperate and subtropical regions of North America, Eurasia, and North Africa from sea level to 11,000 ft (3,300 m).

Habitat: Very broad, but generally in wet alkaline soils in woodlands, scrublands, grasslands, limestone pavement, dune slacks, and marshes.

Many members of this ancient and widespread group are common and familiar Old World wildflowers. Only one species—the Giant Helleborine, *Epipactis gigantea*—occurs naturally in North America, and other members of the genus, notably *E. helleborine*, have become naturalized in the New World following widespread introductions. A number of species rely extensively on symbiotic fungi associated with the roots for nutriment, and occasional specimens of at least one—the Violet Helleborine, *E. purpurata*—are completely lacking in chlorophyll. In such plants the stems and leaves all appear pinkish purple and the flowers are white. Natural hybrids are known for several species.

Cultivation

Helleborines are frost tolerant and can be grown outdoors in full or partial sun in most temperate climates in beds, rock gardens, or well-watered pots. The substratum or potting medium should contain a high proportion of well-mixed leaf mold or peat substitute and should not be allowed to dry out. Repotting or splitting of plants should take place in spring before growth gets underway.

Compared with other members of the genus, *Epipactis gigantea* is a relatively large plant with flowers measuring about 1.8 to 2 inches (4.6–5 cm) across. This native of northwestern America ranges from southern Canada to Mexico.

Epipactis helleborine

The Broad-leaved Helleborine is Europe's most common and widespread wild orchid species. It grows in lightly wooded habitats on base-rich soils and other limestone habitats in all parts of that continent and as far south as northwestern Africa. It has become naturalized in temperate North America, where it is sometimes regarded as a weed.

At first glance it is unspectacular, with a whorl of five to nine ovate dark green leaves and a tall, slightly bent, flower spike; but the small pinkish green flowers have a subdued charm. Cultivated varieties show much greater variation in color. The flowers are normally pollinated by wasps, although self-pollination can also occur.

Cultivation

This common species is incredibly easy to grow in temperate gardens with alkaline soil. It prefers regular watering and light shade and will benefit from a regular dressing with compost or manure, but it can often be left entirely to its own devices and may spread aggressively under the right conditions.

Classification

Epipactis helleborine (Linnaeus) Crantz 1769.

Epipactis helleborine

Eria

DATA

Number of Species: About 500.

Classification: *Eria* Lindley 1825; tribe Epidendreae, subtribe Eriinae.

Form: Highly variable, from compact tufted plants to large erect or creeping forms, with or without pseudobulbs. One to several leaves arise from a stem that may be stout and fleshy or reedlike and up to 40 in (100 cm) long. Flowers are borne singly or on racemes that vary greatly in form. The flowers all have eight pollinia and the lip is usually three-lobed. Many species are covered with fine hairs, giving them a woolly appearance.

Distribution: Tropical regions of Asia and Australasia, from India and China to the Pacific islands.

Habitat: Humid lowlands of the hot tropics.

A complex and diverse group, allied to *Dendrobium*, the *Eria* orchids are united by the arrangement of pollinia and the characteristic form of the lip. Superficially, they can appear completely unrelated. The flowers of many are unspectacular to say the least.

Cultivation

Most of the relatively few species in regular cultivation require warm, humid conditions year round, but with such a large and diverse group there are plenty of exceptions. *Eria* species can be grown in free-draining pots or hanging baskets; those with a creeping habit can be mounted on slabs. The plants should usually be placed in bright sunlight, watered regularly, and fed with dilute (half-strength) balanced fertilizer, with a short period of rest at the end of the active growth season. Repotting and splitting should take place only when the plants reach full size.

Eria acervata is a pseudobulbous epiphyte from the eastern Himalayas to Indochina.

Eria densa

A sturdy plant in which cylindrical pseudobulbs give rise to up to four long, slightly fleshy leaves with a pronounced midrib. Compared to the robustness of the stems and leaves, the flowers are extraordinarily delicate—each less than 0.25 inches (6 mm) across and bloom in dense racemose inflorescences (hence the name) up to 7 inches (18 cm) long. The even-sized sepals and petals have a lightly frosted appearance and range from creamy white to delicate pink. In the wild the species grows in Thailand, the Malay Peninsula, and on the islands of Sumatra and Borneo.

Cultivation

Eria densa requires intermediate to warm conditions and strong partial or dappled sunlight. A humid greenhouse is ideal, although in temperate climates the plant will need to be brought indoors in winter. The plant should be potted in freely draining fir-bark compost mixed with sphagnum moss. Regular watering and feeding will encourage vigorous growth.

Classification

Eria densa Ridley 1896.

Eria densa

Eulophia

DATA

Number of Species: About 250.

Classification: *Eulophia* Robert Brown Ex Lindley 1821; tribe Cymbidieae, subtribe Cyrtopodiinae.

Form: Swollen undergrowth rhizomes or pseudobulbs give rise to very long pleated leaves of variable width and long or tall branched or unbranched racemose inflorescences that bear ornate, usually colorful flowers in clusters of 12 to about 150.

Distribution: Tropical America, Africa, Asia, and northern Australia, with the greatest diversity of species in Africa.

Habitat: Very varied, mostly terrestrial but occasionally epiphytic in habitats from sand dunes and swampy lowlands to deserts, forests, and montane grasslands.

This large and diverse genus has an enormous natural distribution and its members occupy as broad a range of habitats as any orchid group. A few species are saphrophytic, meaning they acquire nutriment from decomposing organic material instead of or in addition to that produced in their own tissues by photosynthesis. Some members of the group are deciduous, shedding their leaves in the fall, while others retain their foliage all year round.

Cultivation

Those *Eulophia* species that produce pseudobulbs are relatively easy to grow potted in standard free-draining terrestrial orchid compost mix. They require regular watering and annual repotting. The tuberous root species are more difficult to maintain, needing a careful regime of watering teamed with excellent drainage to prevent waterlogging. Appropriate temperature and light conditions vary considerably depending on the species.

Eulophia stenopetala is a terrestrial orchid from central Bhutan in South Asia. In cultivation it blooms in the fall.

Flickingeria

DATA

Number of Species: About 70.

Classification: *Flickingeria* A. D. Hawkes 1961; tribe Dendrobieae, subtribe Dendrobiinae.

Form: Stems arise directly from a creeping rhizome. The stems may be branching, erect, or pendulous and are sheathed with scale leaves arising at the internodes. The terminal internodes swell to form pseudobulbs. The flowers are creamy white to pink with a bearded lip.

Distribution: Asia, the islands of the Indo-Pacific and Australia.

Habitat: Epiphytic on trees and shrubs.

These tropical epiphytes have a rather muddled history. The genus was originally known as *Desmotrichum* and was then reclassified as part of the huge group *Dendrobium*. The new genus *Flickingeria* was created in 1961 to accommodate all the former *Desmotrichum* species as well as two that were previously classified in the genus *Ephemeranthera*. The flowers are strikingly beautiful and often produced in profusion, but each bloom is very short lived—most last less than one day. Many species bloom all year round.

Cultivation

Flickingeria orchids require year-round warmth and bright dappled light. They may be planted in a pot or basket with free-draining bark and charcoal mixed with a little chopped sphagnum moss to retain moisture. Alternatively, they may be mounted on a mossy slab of tree fern or bark. When grown under seasonal conditions the plants should be watered and fed regularly during the growing season and rested in winter. They should be repotted in spring and may be divided for propagation at the same time.

Found in many parts of Southeast Asia from Malaysia to the Philippines, *Flickingeria fimbriata* is an epiphyte that grows along rivers and streams at elevations of 650 to 4,300 feet (200–1,300 m).

Galeandra

DATA

Number of Species: About 26.

Classification: *Galeandra* Lindley 1830; tribe Cymbidieae, subtribe Cyrtopodiinae.

Form: In most species, long narrow veined leaves sprout from the nodes of long cylindrical pseudobulbs. The flowers appear on branching inflorescences. The sepals and petals are elongate and pointed and form an erect fan behind the large tubular or cornucopia-shaped lip, which comes to a point or spur at the base. The lip is usually pink or white.

Distribution: Central and South America from Mexico to Bolivia.

Habitat: Most species are epiphytic on trees and shrubs, from sea level to about 1,700 ft (500 m). A few hardier species grow attached to rocky outcrops or on steep ground at higher elevations.

Named for the shape of the anthers (*galea* is Greek for "helmet"), these striking showy orchids are also know colloquially as hooded orchids. The tubular lower lip forms a bell- or hoodlike structure that encloses the anthers and offers shelter to pollinating insects. One species—the pale, apparently saprophytic, and Critically Endangered *Galeandra bicarinata* (synonym *G. beryichii*)—occurs naturally in Florida.

Cultivation

Galeandra orchids can be grown in pots or baskets under intermediate temperature conditions and in indirect light. They should be potted in a light bark and moss mixture. They need plenty of water during the growing season and benefit from high humidity and good air movement. Watering should be reduced a little as the flowers appear and tapered off still more in the winter, when a regular light misting is all that is required.

Galeandra dives is typical of the genus and is similar to a number of other related species. It is found from Costa Rica south through Venezuela to Brazil.

Galeandra batemanii

This rare native of Mexico, Belize, Guatemala, Honduras, and Nicaragua is named for the 19th-century English plant collector and orchid enthusiast James Bateman. It grows as an epiphyte in wet evergreen forests at moderate altitudes up to 3,700 feet (1,100 m). It blooms in the spring and summer. The flowers are roughly 1.3 inches (3 cm) across, and the tubular lip is a delicate lilac pink; the sepals and petals are reddish brown. *Galeandra batemanii* is very similar in form and color to the larger *G. baueri*, which is supposed to be larger and prefers warmer conditions. Some but by no means all authorities prefer to classify the two as the same species.

Cultivation

Galeandra batemanii requires intermediate conditions and shade. After flowering, watering should be reduced and feed suspended. The leaves turn yellow and drop. The plant should be rested in a cool but humid, frost-free situation until signs of regrowth appear in spring.

Classification

Galeandra batemanii Rolfe 1892.

Galeandra batemanii

Gastrochilus

DATA

Number of Species: About 20.

Classification: *Gastrochilus* David Don 1825; tribe Vandeae, subtribe Sarcanthinae.

Form: Most species are compact fan-shaped plants, lacking pseudobulbs and bearing fleshy leaves and waxy flowers. The sepals and petals are of approximately equal size, and the lip forms a fleshy, sometimes ornate pouch. The flowers vary in color, but most are white, cream, or yellow with pink, red, or purple spots or blotches.

Distribution: South and East Asia from India to the Malay and Indonesian archipelagos.

Habitat: Epiphytic on trees and shrubs.

Several members of the group were previously classified within the now defunct genus *Saccolabium*. Incidentally, the generic names *Gastrochilus* and *Saccolabium* describe identical features—the pouchlike lower lip. (*Gastro* means "stomach" in Greek, while *chelis* means "lip"; *saccus* is Latin for "bag," and *labium* is Latin for "lip.") The group's taxonomy remains a little muddled, with many species having one or more synonyms so some sources list as many as 45 members of the genus.

Cultivation

Most species fare best on slab mounts or in baskets in moderate to bright light at intermediate temperature—a bright windowsill or greenhouse is ideal in temperate climates. The few high-altitude species prefer cooler conditions. All species require regular watering all year round and should be fed in the growing season with dilute fertilizer.

This hybrid is *Gastrochilus calceolaris* 'Vista.'
The species originates from South and Southeast Asia.

Gastrochilus acutifolius

A native of northern India and Nepal, *Gastrochilus acutifolius* (*Saccolabium acutifolium*) is adapted to life at altitude in the foothills of the Himalayas, where it grows attached to forks in tree trunks and branches. The leaves are long and leathery, and the small flowers bloom in flat densely clustered inflorescences. They have the appearance of textured marzipan or sugar decorations. The sepals and petals are greenish yellow, while the ornate pouchlike lip is white with pink and yellow spots. The flowers are highly fragranced and long lasting.

Cultivation

A cool-growing species, *G. acutifolius* is best cultivated in a basket of free-draining epiphytic compost or mounted on a tree-fern block. It requires year-round watering and feeding, although quantities of both water and fertilizer should be reduced after flowering.

Classification

Gastrochilus acutifolius (Lindley) Kuntze 1891.

Gastrochilus acutifolius

Gongora

DATA

Number of Species: About 65.

Classification: *Gongora* Ruiz & Pavon 1794/8; tribe Cymbidiae, subtribe Stanhopeinae.

Form: Two to three veined leaves up to 12 in (30 cm) long arise from ribbed, egg-shaped pseudobulbs with fine white aerial roots, while inflorescences sprout from their bases. The inflorescences bear many small upside-down flowers on highly curved pedicels (flower stalks). The large lip has two sections: the hypochile and the epichile. The dorsal sepal and petals are small. The large lateral sepals curl back on themselves.

Distribution: Central and South America from Mexico south to Bolivia and Peru, with Colombia as the center of diversity.

Habitat: Many species grow on trees or rock faces. Some root themselves in ant mounds in damp forests at low to moderate elevations from sea level to about 6,300 ft (1,900 m).

These unusual orchids are named for Antonio Caballero y Gongora, viceroy of what was the Spanish colony of New Granada, now Ecuador and Colombia, during the 18th century when the group was first scientifically described. The genus is due for a taxonomic review in the light of molecular evidence, and it is likely that several species will be hived off into new genera. The flowers of *Gongora* orchids are pollinated by male bees of the genus *Euglossa*. Each species forms a mutually beneficial relationship with a different species of *Euglossa* bee. Only the male bees are attracted to the flowers, which are strongly scented. A number of hybrids have been produced between *Gongora* species and members of other genera.

Cultivation

The pendent or trailing character of the inflorescences means that *Gongora* species are shown to best effect in hanging baskets. The plants should be potted in standard free-draining epiphyte mix and watered regularly. The aerial roots should be misted and not allowed to dry out. All species benefit from regular feeds throughout the year.

Gongora pleiochroma is a South American species that ranges from Colombia to Peru and possibly Guyana and Brazil.

Gongora galeata

A Mexican endemic, *Gongora galeata* grows as an epiphyte on trees in humid tropical forests. Up to six pendulous inflorescences, each consisting of as many as 20 strange-looking, highly scented brownish yellow flowers, bloom in succession from each individual pseudobulb. The continuity of flowering throughout the summer makes this a popular species for growers.

Cultivation

Gongora galeata orchids are best planted in baskets in a fibrous compost mix with chopped sphagnum moss and bark chippings, and hung where they will receive intermediate conditions of light and temperature. They do well in greenhouses in temperate climates. The plants require copious water during the growing season and should be fed at least once a month during the growing season. Watering can be reduced over the winter months but should not be suspended altogether. The plants should be repotted in spring, at which time clustered pseudobulbs may be split for propagation.

Classification

Gongora galeata (Lindley) Reichenbach f. 1854.

Gongora galeata

Habenaria

Number of Species: About 600.

Classification: *Habenaria*
Willdenow 1805; tribe
Orchideae, subtribe
Habenariinae.

Form: Terrestrial orchids with
tubers or fleshy roots. Leaves
are smooth, sheathlike up the
stem, a few basal. Inflorescence
is a terminal raceme with one
flower, usually green or white,
some yellow, orange, pink, or
red. The dorsal sepal, along
with the petals, forms a hood
over the column; lateral sepals
are reflexed or deflexed. Lip is
three-lobed or toothed, entire,
with a long or short spur. The
column may be long or short,
with two clavate or pyriform
pollinia.

Distribution: South America,
southern China, Africa, Asia,
and Vietnam.

Habitat: Mainly tropical and
temperate grasslands, often
near streams or rivers; also
forest floors and on rocks.

The greatest concentration of *Habenaria* species is in tropical
South America, Asia, and Africa, often in damp to slightly boggy
grasslands, hence the common name for the genus of bog orchids.

They are deciduous plants and die down after the flowering process,
leaving a fleshy tuber beneath the ground. The flowers frequently have a
delicate and bizarre structure and may emit a sweet scent in the evening
to attract moths, which act as pollinators.

The name *Habenaria* is from the Latin *habena* meaning "reins"
or "straps," alluding to the straplike lip divisions of the lip. Within this
large genus are some very attractive terrestrials that vary in both
structure and color.

Cultivation

Disa culture has been put forward as a solution to growing these plants.
The aim is a rich porous compost that will be water retentive during the
vital growing season but able to become dryer once the tubers go into
their rest and maturation period. While resting, the plants must have
sufficient moisture to stop desiccation of the tubers. Grow in clay pots
with crock pieces in the base. Use six parts bark, three parts coarse peat
substitute, and one part perlite. Really first-class drainage is essential.
Give good light once new growth is seen. Only give liberal amounts of
water to begin with, increasing as the plant grows. Start off in the
greenhouse and place outside on warm days. Keep only just moist as the
plant dies back. Once all signs of green have gone the tubers may be
taken carefully from the pot and divided before being repotted. Keep
newly potted tubers just moist until the next year's new growth appears.

Habenaria trifida occurs from Mexico to tropical America.

Habenaria rhodocheila

This orchid occurs in Thailand, Indochina, southern China, Malaysia, and the Philippines, where it often grows in leaf litter between rocks in evergreen forest at low to moderate altitudes.

The most distinctive feature of this species is the lobed lip which comes in various shades of scarlet, orange, or yellow. It is a terrestrial orchid with bulbous fleshy roots, a stem 4 to 12 inches (10–30 cm) long with one or two leaves below and three to four leaves above. The leaves are linear to lanceolate and grow to 2.5 to 5 inches (6–13 cm) long. The inflorescence is densely covered with up to 15 flowers. The sepals and petals are green to greenish, and the dorsal sepal and petal form a hood. The lip is four-lobed, the side lobes being oblique. There is a slender spur 1.5 to 2 inches (4–5 cm) long. The column is oblique.

Cultivation

The aim is to achieve a rich porous compost that will be water retentive during the vital growing season but able to become dryer once the tubers go into their rest and maturation period. While resting, the plants must have sufficient moisture to stop desiccation of the tubers. Grow in clay pots with crock pieces in the base. Use six parts bark, three parts coarse peat substitute, and one part perlite. Really first-class drainage is essential. Give good light once new growth is seen. Only give liberal amounts of water to begin with, increasing as the plant grows. Start off in the greenhouse and place outside on warm days. Keep only just moist as the plant dies back. Once all signs of green have gone the tubers may be taken carefully from the pot and divided before being repotted. Keep newly potted tubers just moist until the next year's new growth appears.

Classification

Habenaria rhodocheila Hance 1856.

Habenaria rhodocheila

Ida

DATA

Number of Species: About 42.

Classification: *Ida* A. Ryan & Oakeley 2003; tribe Maxillarieae, subtribe Lycastinae.

Form: A variable genus that comprises plants either with large pseudobulbs that are pale green, smooth, ovoid, bearing large plicate leaves up to 39 in (1 m) long and 8 in (20 cm) wide or those with narrow, tapering, cylindrical pseudobulbs and narrow leaves no more than 15 in (38 cm) long and 1.6 in (4 cm) wide. Roots have thick spongy cells (velamen) on the outside and are hairy.

Distribution: Caribbean islands and Brazil (one species); Colombia, Ecuador, Peru, Venezuela, Bolivia.

Habitat: Most grow at altitudes from 5,580 to 8,850 ft (1,700–2,700 m), some to 11,800 ft (3,600 m); epiphytic, lithophytic, and terrestrial in light woodland or, at higher altitudes, open grassland in full sun.

This genus was separated from *Lycaste* on the basis of distribution, gross and microscopic floral and vegetative structure, color, fragrance, pollination biology, and molecular studies.

One species, *Ida dyeriana*, has pendulous flowers but the remainder have campanulate or semi-campanulate flowers on erect to horizontal scapes. Flowering occurs in a single episode per year, all the flowers appearing at the same time, usually with one (occasionally two) flower(s) per inflorescence. The flower colors range from pale green or greenish yellow to white; there is a pale beige group and an important group with large plants and flowers with green to olive tepals and green to brick red lips. The majority have a large, fleshy, heavily ridged callus, falcate sepals, and a distinct nectar-containing mentum. The lips are often heavily fringed. There is little variation in the amyl-like fragrance, which is more common at dusk or during the night. Pollination is thought to be by night-flying bees.

Artificial hybrids with *Lycaste* and *Anguloa* have been made.

Cultivation

Most *Ida* species can be grown in intermediate conditions with plenty of light; in northern temperate climates only slight shade is needed in the height of summer, and none in winter. A winter night temperature of 59°F (15°C), rising to 86°F (30°C) during the summer daytime, with 50 to 70 percent humidity and good air movement, suits them well. Grow in a pot or a basket in a mix of one part perlite to one part sphagnum moss. Water frequently during the growing season and do not allow to dry out completely when resting.

Ida reichenbachii is from Peru.

(Text and photos Henry Oakeley)

Ida locusta

Found only in Peru, where it is common, this is a dramatic species. It grows in light humid woodland, epiphytically or terrestrially in thick leaf mold, and lithophytically on boulders and cliffs, sometimes in full sun. It is found at altitudes between 6,230 and 8,850 feet (1,900 and 2,700 m) and usually flowers around August to November. When undisturbed it forms huge colonies up to 330 feet (100 m) across.

The flowers—which usually number two to five—are dark green with a white fringe to the lip. They drip with nectar, emitting a strong fragrance of apples at night, which attracts swarms of moths. The pseudobulbs are ovoid to pyriform, 3.4 x 2 x 1.4 inches (85 x 50 x 35 mm), bearing three to four narrow plicate leaves up to 30 inches (75 cm) long and 3 inches (8 cm) wide. The flowers are 2.8 inches (7 cm) wide and are borne singly (occasionally in pairs) on inflorescences up to 20 inches (50 cm) long. In nature they often point downward at first and then arch upward.

Cultivation

Ida locusta needs to be grown in intermediate conditions with plenty of light; in northern temperate climates only slight shade is needed in the height of summer, and none in winter. A winter night temperature of 59°F (15°C), rising to 86°F (30°C) during the summer daytime, with 50 to 70 percent humidity and good air movement, suits them well. Grow in a pot or a basket in a mix of one part perlite to one part sphagnum moss. In a basket the flowers may come out through the sides. It experiences heavy rainfalls in the growing season in its habitat and never dries out, so in cultivation this should be copied—water frequently during the growing season and do not allow it to dry out completely when resting. The leaves may stay on the plant for three years.

Classification

Ida locusta (Reichenbach f.) A. Ryan & Oakeley 2003.

Ida locusta

Jumellea

DATA

Number of Species: About 60.

Classification: *Jumellea* Schlechter 1914; tribe Vandeae, subtribe Angraecinae.

Form: Small to medium epiphytic or lithophytic plants with stems that are very short to long (rarely branched). The leaves are few to numerous, arranged in two rows, and two-lobed at their apex. The inflorescence bears a single white or greenish white flower. The sepals and petals are nearly similar, with the lateral sepals joined at the base beneath a short spur. The lip is entire, the callus linear to tapering, and the column short and fleshy.

Distribution: Madagascar, Comoros and Mascarene islands; two species in Africa.

Habitat: From sea level up to 8,100 ft (2,500 m), found growing on moss-covered rocks and stones or clinging to coarse bark and tree branches.

The genus *Jumellea* is named for the botanist Dr. Henri Jumelle. Flowers are fragrant, generally white, some with a hint of green. In Victorian times the dried foliage of *Jumellea fragrans* was imported into England and France to be made into the fragrant drink "Faham Tea"; it contains the chemical coumarin and is said to have a sedating effect.

Cultivation

With their spreading roots, jumelleas can be untidy plants and they have a tendency to form clumps. Grow on large pieces of tree fern or coarse blocks or slabs, which allow the roots to grip and give them room to spread. Some species grow upright, while others tend to droop or hang down. They can also be grown in pans and baskets.

Because of the wide range of habitats preferred by different species (from mountainsides to forested areas), the range of temperatures required in cultivation varies from cool to warm. Provide high humidity with good light to slight shade, and water well while growing. There is no set time of flowering for some of the species.

Jumellea sagittata is an evergreen white-flowered species from central Madagascar.

Laelia

DATA

Number of Species: About 21.

Classification: *Laelia* Lindley 1831; tribe Epidendreae, subtribe Laeliinae.

Form: Epiphytic, lithophytic, and terrestrial with a creeping rhizome. Pseudobulbs ovoid or cylindrical, bearing one or two fleshy or leathery leaves at the apex. The racemose inflorescence bears one to a few flowers. Flowers large and showy, orange, scarlet, white, pink, yellow, or purple. Sepals and petals are spreading, flat, or undulate. Sepals are more or less equal; Petals are similar but often wider than the sepals. The lip is free or lightly joined at the base of the column. Column is long with a toothed apex and eight pollinia.

Distribution: Mexico, Central America, northern South America, West Indies.

Habitat: Lowlands, highlands, open fields, pastures, pine forests, rocks, other wet- or dry-type forests.

Until recently, the genus *Laelia* contained a number of species from Brazil. These have now been transferred to the genus *Sophronitis* as a result of DNA studies. However, they are still often sold as *Laelia* species—commercial horticulture is often slow to react to scientific reclassification. About 11 *Laelia* species come from Mexico, with the remainder from more tropical parts of Central and northern South America and the West Indies.

Laelia (with eight pollinia) is closely allied to the genus *Cattleya* (four pollinia) and there are many intergeneric hybrids in cultivation.

Cultivation

The Mexican species of *Laelia* require slightly cooler conditions generally than the more tropical species that remain in the genus (and the original Brazilian *Laelia* species now transferred to *Sophronitis*). They also need to be kept drier in winter.

In general *Laelia* should be cultivated as for orchids in the genus *Cattleya*. Grow them in pots containing a good open medium, at warm to intermediate temperatures. Provide shade and high humidity during growth. Mexican species, such as *L. anceps*, can be grown mounted on blocks or rafts or in baskets. Water well when roots are growing and mist while at rest.

Laelia flava (Sophronitis crispata) occurs in the state of Minas Gerais, Brazil.

Laelia anceps

An epiphytic or lithophytic orchid that has ovate pseudobulbs clustered or spaced on a creeping rhizome. The single leaves borne at the pseudobulb apex are 6 to 9 inches (15 to 23 cm) long, lanceolate, leathery, and glossy green. The inflorescence is 24 to 30 inches (60 to 75 cm) long, erect, and produces two to five fragrant showy flowers that are pale rose to dark reddish purple in color. The lip is three-lobed in the middle, with the throat tinged with yellow and white, and veined with purple.

Cultivation

This Mexican species is normally found on rocks, tree trunks, and branches. Good drainage is essential. It is best grown in a basket using medium to coarse bark plus perlag or chopped sphagnum moss for moisture retention. Give the plant plenty of water when the roots are growing. During the dormant period keep it dry and cool, but maintain bright light and mist the plant. Maintain good ventilation but low humidity at all times.

Classification

Laelia anceps Lindley 1835.

Laelia anceps

Laelia (Sophronitis) harpophylla

This Brazilian species, which occurs from Minas Gerais to Espírito Santo, is an example of a former *Laelia* species that has recently been reclassified as a species of *Sophronitis*. However, it is still available from growers under its original name so is included here as an example.

It is an epiphyte with slender, stemlike, clustered, erect pseudobulbs, between 5 and 18 inches (13 and 45 cm) tall. The single leaf is ligulate, lanceolate, and leathery. The inflorescence is equal to or shorter than the leaves and bears up to seven flowers. The flowers are long lasting, orange, 2 to 3.5 inches (5–8 cm) across and have a paler margin on the lip. The lip is three-lobed.

Cultivation

For this typical Brazilian species use a mixture of fine bark, perlite, charcoal, and sphagnum moss to produce a compact but free-draining compost. Brazilian species such as this need to be firm in the pot and the canes and pseudobulbs may need tying to keep them erect. Water well during the period of root growth. Provide high humidity with partial shade—mist on warm days and during the rest period; always provide good ventilation and air movement.

Classification

Laelia harpophylla Reichenbach f. 1873. (accepted synonym *Sophronitis harpophylla* (Reichenbach f. 2000).

Laelia (Sophronitis) harpophylla

Other *Laelia* Species

Laelia autumnalis
from Mexico.

Laelia rubescens from
Mexico to Panama.

Laelia speciosa
from Mexico.

Leptotes

DATA

Number of Species: No more than 6.

Classification: *Leptotes* Lindley. 1833; tribe Epidendreae, subtribe Laeliinae.

Form: Tends to form clumps. Small epiphyte with a creeping rhizome and stemlike, cylindrical, apically unifoliate pseudobulbs bearing a single erect fleshy leaf. The inflorescence is a slender terminal raceme with short bracts and one to few flowers. The flowers are medium size, spreading with virtually similar free sepals and petals. The lip is free, three-lobed; side lobes have a short claw, midlobe is longer. The column is fleshy, erect, and short with six waxy pollinia (four large and two small).

Distribution: Argentina, Brazil, and Paraguay.

Habitat: Subtropical rain-forest to mountainous habitats. Grows with bright but shaded light, humid conditions, and good air movement.

The name *Leptotes* derives from the Greek *leptotes* (meaning "delicateness" or "delicate appearance"). It alludes to the attractive and delicate nature of *Leptotes* species. With its fragrant white and pink flowers up to 2 inches (5 cm) across, *L. bicolor* is perhaps the best known of this small genus. The seed pods of *Leptotes* have been used in Brazil to flavor ice cream and other confectionery.

Cultivation

Leptotes species must be grown on bark or a tree-fern slab. They like a bright but shady position that has good air movement and high humidity. Water well in the growing season. After flowering has taken place, reduce the amount of water given, providing just sufficient to prevent dehydration. Do not allow the pseudobulbs to shrivel. When growing in pots, use a mix of one-half fine bark and one-half sphagnum moss. Add polystyrene beads, stones, or crock in the bottom of the pot to aid drainage.

A species of subtropical rain forests, *Leptotes bicolor* is found in southern Brazil and Paraguay.

Liparis

DATA

Number of Species: About 250.

Classification: *Liparis* Richard 1817; tribe Malaxideae, subtribe Liparindinae.

Form: Terrestrial and lithophytic, less commonly epiphytic. Stems arise from pseudobulbs or corms bearing one to several plicate, thin-textured leaves that have sheathing bases. The inflorescence is erect with few to many small yellowish green or purplish flowers. The sepals are free and spreading, the petals often linear. The lip is the largest part of the bloom. The column is long, mostly elongate, with four waxy and ovoid pollinia in two pairs.

Distribution: Malaysia, Sri Lanka, China, Pacific islands, temperate and sub-Mediterranean Europe, North America.

Habitat: Mainly terrestrial in wet marshy areas.

This large genus of orchids occurs almost throughout the world. Even the single species *Liparis loeselii* occurs in central and eastern Canada, north-central and eastern United States, Europe, and central Asia. Typically they are found in wet montane forests at altitudes of 2,000 to 9,800 feet (600 to 3,000 m), where they grow in cool humid conditions on alkaline to neutral soils, in full sun or partial shade. A number of them are very rare, and collection of plants from the wild is illegal in many areas.

The name *Liparis* is derived from the Greek (liparos) meaning greasy, shiny looking, referring to the leaves.

Cultivation

These orchids are not easy to grow and are not ideal for the amateur grower. *Liparis* species from tropical and subtropical regions require shaded conditions in the intermediate temperature range and live sphagnum moss as the medium. A winter temperature of 54 to 59°F (12-15 °C) is required. Other more temperate species can be grown outdoors in a specially prepared humid and cool peat substitute or bog garden that is always moist and exposed to a mixture of sun and shade.

Liparis reflexa is a native of southeastern Queensland and New South Wales, Australia.

Lycaste

DATA

Number of Species: 32.

Classification: *Lycaste* Lindley 1843; tribe Maxillarieae, subtribe Lycastinae.

Form: Sympodial, with ovoid pseudobulbs from the base of which the new growths appear. Two to five large plicate leaves emerge from the pseudobulb apex; three to five sheathing leaves occur from around the base but are lost as the bulb matures. The many inflorescences are usually horizontal to erect, each bearing one (occasionally two) flower(s).

Distribution: Mexico, Central America, Colombia, Ecuador, Peru, Venezuela, Bolivia, Brazil.

Habitat: Usually epiphytic in shade and near water at lower altitudes, becoming lithophytic and terrestrial in light woodland and open grassland with full sun at high altitudes, even in the same species.

When he published *Lycaste plana* a year before he described the genus, Lindley said of the name *Lycaste*, "A fanciful name, Lycaste was a beautiful woman." He and Paxton later wrote, "*Lycaste* Lindl. Lycaste was a beautiful woman of Sicily." Lycaste lived in the time of classical Greece in Drepanum, Sicily. She was the wife of Butes and was nicknamed "Venus" because of her great beauty. At the same time as Lindley separated *Lycaste* from *Maxillaria* he also separated out *Paphinia* from the same genus. *Paphinia* is another name for Aphrodite (Venus), whose main temple was at Paphus in Cyprus.

The yellow-flowered *Lycaste* species are mainly found in Mexico and countries to its immediate south, although *L. macrobulbon* and *L. campbellii* extend into the territory of the *L. macrophylla* group in South America. Members of the yellow-flowered group produce pheromones that induce mating activity in male euglossine bees, which then visit the flowers. The Central American species contain some of the prettiest and smallest plants in the genus, with very local distribution, while *L. macrophylla* and related species are found from Mexico to Brazil and are very variable.

In the species from habitats that have a long dry season the plants are deciduous for up to three months before new growth and flowering commence, and in these species the leaf abscission point on the pseudobulb contains sharp spines.

The majority of lycastes are fragrant, the yellow-flowered ones having a pleasant smell of cloves and similar fragrances when in sunshine. Those with an affinity to *L. macrophylla*, including the South American yellow-flowered species, smell of old fashioned soap (with the

Lycaste guatemalensis from Guatemala.

exception of the odorless *L. skinneri*). The stimulus to flower-bud production may be a period of relative dryness after maturation of the new pseudobulb.

Cultivation

Although found from between sea level and 9,200 feet (2,800 m), the growing conditions for the plants are more similar than the wide range of altitudes would suggest. With the exception of *L. skinneri*, which needs cool conditions, and *L. macrobulbon* and *L. campbellii*, which need warm conditions, they grow best in an intermediate greenhouse with light shade and humidity between 50 and 70 percent. Cooler conditions in winter are tolerated, but the plants come into growth and flower later and produce smaller pseudobulbs. Temperatures from 59°F (15°C) at night in winter to a maximum of 86°F (30°C) in the daytime in summer are best, although higher temperatures are tolerated if the plants are well watered and there is strong air movement over the leaves.

They grow well in pots with a well-drained compost of 50:50 bark or Perlite and sphagnum moss. Water and feed well during the growing season, not allowing them to dry out. When the pseudobulbs have matured and the side leaves have been lost, reduce watering to sufficient to prevent the pseudobulbs from shriveling. Plants that are completely deciduous may not need watering for two months or more. Restart watering when new growth or flower buds are seen.

(Text and photos Henry Oakeley)

Lycaste campbellii grows in moss on large tree trunks at sea level from Panama to Colombia.

Lycaste aromatica

This orchid is epiphytic in light woodland at up to 5,600 feet (1,700 m) in southern Mexico, but it also grows lithophytically in leaf mold on limestone cliffs and boulders. The pseudobulbs are up to 4.3 inches (11 cm) long and produce three apical leaves to 24 inches (60 cm) long and 6 inches (15 cm) wide and up to 20 fragrant yellow flowers 2.4 inches (6 cm) wide. A single flowering occurs between February and June, depending on the clone (in cultivation in northern temperate greenhouses). It is deciduous, since in its habitat there may be no rain for four months. With its spiny pseudobulbs it may be regarded as a cactus for this time, with respect to cultivation.

Cultivation

Give only slight shade with good air movement, and water and feed frequently while the plant is growing. When the side leaves have fallen off, stop watering. Until the new growth and flower buds appear, allow the compost to dry out and water only if the pseudobulbs start to shrivel.

Classification

Lycaste aromatica (Graham) Lindley 1842

Lycaste aromatica

Lycaste dowiana

An epiphytic orchid, *Lycaste dowiana* grows in humid cloud forest in light shade at 2,600 to 4,900 feet (800 to 1,500 m) in Central America (Guatemala, Honduras, Costa Rica, and Nicaragua). It was named for Captain J. M. Dow, who transported many plant hunters from Europe to Latin America in the mid-19th century.

It is one of the smallest of the lycastes, with pseudobulbs 2.4 inches (6 cm) long and leaves that grow to 18 inches (46 cm) long and 4 inches (10 cm) wide. It has single flowers, 2.4 inches (6 cm) wide, on inflorescences 1.6 to 2.8 inches (4–7 cm) long. It flowers all summer (May to September) in northern temperate greenhouses, with a succession of well-shaped flowers, up to five at a time. The sepals are brown, and the petals and lip are cream, the latter having a horseshoe-shaped pattern of pink dots around the midlobe.

It is a particularly useful parent of small-growing, repeat-flowering hybrids, especially when crossed with large-flowered winter-blooming species. The brown coloration is composed of red pigment on a green background, and many of its offspring inherit this attractive red color.

Cultivation

It grows well in a free-draining perlite and sphagnum compost. Water regularly through the summer, but since it is not deciduous, it should not be allowed to dry out in the winter, although watering may be reduced at this time. It prefers light shade rather than full sun. The flowers do not need staking.

Classification

Lycaste dowiana Endres ex Reichenbach f. 1874.

Lycaste dowiana

Lycaste macrophylla

The Peruvian *Lycaste macrophylla* var. *plana* is the most common form of this species in cultivation. At 3 inches (8 cm), its stem is short, and its flowers are up to 4 inches (10 cm) wide. The pseudobulbs are not spined and measure up to 4.3 inches (11 cm) long, with leaves that grow to 25 inches (63 cm) long and 2.4 inches (6 cm) wide. It has reddish brown sepals, white petals, and a lip with a variable amount of red spotting. Forms with pale green sepals and white petals and lip are also available. They flower erratically through the summer, often with flowers in the winter as well.

Cultivation

These plants are very adaptable to a wide range of growing conditions, tolerating varying degrees of shade and temperature without problems, which explains their success in colonizing a wide range of habitats. However, intermediate temperatures and light shade are best; water and feed freely during the growing season. They are not deciduous until after the new growth is well established, so do not allow the plants to dry out in the winter, although watering should be reduced.

Classification

Lycaste macrophylla (Poeppig & Endlicher) Lindley 1843.

Lycaste macrophylla

Masdevallia

DATA

Number of Species: About 350.

Classification: *Masdevallia* Ruiz and Pavon 1794; tribe Epidendreae, subtribe Pleurothallidinae.

Form: Small tufted epiphytes and lithophytes forming dense clumps. Foliage is glossy green and emerges from a short creeping rhizome. Leaves are fleshy, erect to suberect, and narrow to elliptical. The racemose inflorescence is erect to spreading, bearing a single terminal flower or several flowers, which are variously colored, small to large, and triangular in shape. The sepals are ovate to triangular, fused near base to form a tube, terminating in long or short tails; petals are smaller than sepals. Lip is small, three-lobed or entire. The column is short to arching, with two waxy pollinia.

Distribution: Mexico to Brazil, Bolivia.

Habitat: Mostly cloud forest.

This genus of spectacular orchids is found at its highest concentration in the foothills and highlands of the Andes from Venezuela to Peru, which are typically clothed in cloud forests where heavy dew and copious rain occur daily. *Masdevallia* was named for the 18th-century botanist and physician in the court of Spain, Dr. Jose Masdeval. The genus is closely allied to *Pleurothallis*, *Dracula*, *Dryadella*, and *Trisetella*.

The key characteristic of the genus are the often triangular sepals which form a tube at the base and the tips of which are drawn out into tails, which may be up to 3 to 4 inches (75 to 100 mm) long. In many case these features give an overall triangular shape to the flowers. Flower colors vary from vibrant reds and oranges through darker purple tones to white and green.

Cultivation

To be grown successfully these orchids need a free-draining yet moisture-retentive medium, which can vary from grower to grower. Typically they can be grown in a mixture of fine bark, sphagnum moss, and charcoal. Place polystyrene beans or crocks in the base of the pot for drainage. They grow best in mostly cool, sometimes intermediate, conditions (depending on the species type) with a maximum temperature of 75°F (25°C). High humidity, and a cool air supply are important, with good ventilation to remove excess heat. Water every three to four days to keep the medium moist at all times (but not wet, hence the need for good drainage). Feed once a month with a balanced fertilizer. Proper watering is the key to cultivating these orchids. Propagate by division or seed.

Masdevallia veitchiana 'Angel Frost'

Masdevallia coccinea

With its brightly colored flowers, this spectacular orchid occurs on rocky cliffs at elevations of 7,900 to 9,200 feet (2,400–2,800 m) in the Andes of Colombia and Peru.

Its leaves are clustered, erect, and narrow to oblong. The stem is up to 2.5 inches (6 cm) long and concealed in sheaths. The slender inflorescence is up to 16 inches (41 cm) long, with one flower at its apex. Flowers are large, showy, and variable in color from magenta and purple to yellow or white. The perianth tube is waxy. The dorsal sepal is variable, 1.5 to 3.5 inches (4–9 cm) long, and narrowly triangulate or linear with a slender recurved tail. The lateral sepals are longer than the dorsal sepal, joined in the bottom third, and the outer margins are sickle shaped. The petals are very small, two-lobed at the apex, usually off white in color, and somewhat translucent. The lip is oblong with a rounded apex.

Cultivation

Grow in pots using a well-drained moisture-retentive medium of fine bark mixed with sphagnum moss and charcoal (larger proportions of the first two), with polystyrene beans or crocks at the bottom of the pot to aid drainage. Loosely pack the plant within the compost but do not press down. Maintain high humidity, plenty of air movement, and good light with shade. Water every three or four days (or as the plants warrant) to keep the medium moist but not wet. Feed once a month with a balanced fertilizer. Grow under cool to intermediate temperature conditions.

Classification

Masdevallia coccinea Linden 1842.

Masdevallia coccinea

Masdevallia infracta

This small epiphytic orchid occurs in Brazil and Bolivia, where it grows in montane forests at elevations of 3,600 to 6,500 feet (1,100–2,000 m). *Masdevallia infracta* has erect, glossy, leathery, oblong to lanceolate green leaves arranged in tufts. The inflorescence is erect, three-winged, 10 inches (25 cm) long, and produces one to five flowers. The flowers are variable in color, the insides being purple to dark wine red, and the outsides purplish pink to somber red. The distinctive tails are yellowish white. The lip is linear to slightly fiddle shaped, with the apex spotted reddish brown.

Cultivation

Grow in pots using a well-drained moisture-retentive medium of fine bark mixed with sphagnum moss and charcoal (larger proportions of the first two), with polystyrene beans or crocks at the bottom of the pot to aid drainage. Loosely pack the plant within the compost but do not press down. Maintain high humidity, plenty of air movement, and good light with shade. Water every three or four days (or as the plants warrant) to keep the medium moist but not wet. Feed once a month with a balanced fertilizer. Grow under cool to intermediate temperature conditions.

Classification

Masdevallia infracta Lindley 1833.

Masdevallia infracta

315

Masdevallia tovarensis

This miniature masdevallia is found in mountain regions of Venezuela growing at elevations of 5,250 to 7,900 feet (1,600–2,400 m). The dark green and shiny leaves of *Masdevallia tovarensis* are suberect, clustered together, and elliptical to spoon shaped. The inflorescence is erect to suberect, three-angled, 7.5 inches (19 cm) long, with two bracts at the apex, and bearing one to four flowers. These are long lived and showy—pure white with a purple column that is white at the apex and base, with green ovaries and creamy to yellowish green tails.

Cultivation

Grow in pots using a well-drained moisture-retentive medium of fine bark mixed with sphagnum moss and charcoal (larger proportions of the first two), with polystyrene beans or crocks at the bottom of the pot to aid drainage. Loosely pack the plant within the compost but do not press down. Maintain high humidity, plenty of air movement, and good light with shade. Water every three or four days (or as the plants warrant) to keep the medium moist but not wet. Feed once a month with a balanced fertilizer. Grow under cool to intermediate temperature conditions.

With this species, once the flower has died do not cut off the inflorescence because it will reflower later or the following year.

Classification

Masdevallia tovarensis Reichenbach f. 1849.

Masdevallia tovarensis

Masdevallia veitchiana

This large lithophytic, sometimes terrestrial, orchid occurs in Peru at altitudes from 6,500 to 13,000 feet (2,000–4,000 m), typically on grass-covered rocky slopes exposed to full sun but protected by the taller grasses. It is a large tufted species with pale green leaves up to 6 to 10 inches (15–25 cm) long. The inflorescence is 12 to 19 inches (30–48 cm) tall and produces just a single large and showy flower, 2 to 3 inches (5–7.5 cm) across. The sepals are orange to scarlet and covered in crimson to purple papillae, or hairs. The lateral sepals are larger than the dorsal sepal, and the tails are short and pointing forward. The lip is oblong to oblong-ovate and the column is short and colored white.

Cultivation

Grow in pots using a well-drained moisture-retentive medium of fine bark mixed with sphagnum moss and charcoal (larger proportions of the first two), with polystyrene beans or crocks at the bottom of the pot to aid drainage. Loosely pack the plant within the compost but do not press down. Maintain high humidity, plenty of air movement, and good light with shade. Water every three or four days (or as the plants warrant) to keep the medium moist but not wet. Feed once a month with a balanced fertilizer. Grow under cool to intermediate temperature conditions.

Classification

Masdevallia veitchiana Reichenbach f. 1868.

Masdevallia veitchiana

319

Other *Masdevallia* Species

Masdevallia caloptera from northern Peru.

Masdevallia ferrusii from Ecuador.

Masdevallia sertula from Ecuador.

Masdevallia angulifera from Colombia.

Masdevallia pachyura from Ecuador.

Maxillaria

DATA

Number of Species: About 650.

Classification: *Maxillaria* Ruiz and Pavon 1794; tribe Maxillarieae, subtribe Maxillariinae.

Form: Variable; rhizomatous or tufted. Rhizome short to elongated, creeping and ascending. Pseudobulbs may be hardly visible, small or large, clustered, with one or two leaves at the apex. Inflorescence arises singly or in groups from base of pseudobulb and bears a single flower. Flowers sometimes showy, small or up to 5 in (13 cm) in diameter, in brown, red, yellow, or white. Lip is entire or three-lobed, sessile, and attached to column foot. The disk usually has a distinct callus; four waxy pollinia present.

Distribution: Southern United States to northern Argentina; West Indies.

Habitat: Epiphytic in wet tropical forests, occasionally lithophytic on rock formations, from sea level to 12,300 ft (3,700 m).

One of the largest orchid genera, *Maxillaria* was previously divided into a number of smaller genera, such as *Ornithidium* and *Camaridium*, but these are not regarded as valid at this time. The name *Maxillaria* comes from the Latin *maxilla* ("jaw"), a reference to the lip and column, which look like the jaws of an insect.

The range of species within the genus is wide—from Florida to southern South America. Just a single species, *M. crassifolia*, is found in Florida, extending through Central America well into South America and the West Indies, although it is less common in Florida than elsewhere. Some of the smaller species grow in tufts and are botanically termed "caespitose."

Cultivation

These orchids require cool to intermediate temperature conditions. They can be grown in pots or baskets or on bark pieces. For small species, place in a fine open bark substrate with a little added perlite to maintain free-draining conditions. Alternatively, grow on small bark pieces with a pad of sphagnum moss around the roots. For the larger species, use pots or baskets containing free-draining light to medium bark chip with added sphagnum moss to retain moisture. In both cases, keep in moderately shaded humid conditions with good air movement. Water them well while growing. When the pseudobulbs have matured, give less water, but never allow the plant to dry out.

Maxillaria crassifolia is found from southern Florida to southern South America.

Maxillaria lepidota

This large epiphytic herb occurs in damp forests in Colombia, Venezuela, Peru, and Ecuador. Its pseudobulbs are clustered, ovoid to cylindrical, with membranous sheaths, and grow to 2 inches (5 cm) tall and 0.6 inches (1.5 cm) in diameter. Each pseudobulb bears a single linear, ligulate, suberect leaf at its apex. The leaves are 14 inches (36 cm) long and 0.75 inches (2 cm) wide, including a folded petiolate base. The inflorescence is 5 inches (13 cm) long and bears a single spiderlike flower. The sepals and petals are yellow, with the base splashed with red. The lip is fleshy, three-lobed, creamy yellow, and marked maroon along its dorsal axis, with the side lobes erect. The column is short and slightly curved.

Cultivation

Grow at intermediate temperatures in pots containing fine bark with small amounts of sphagnum moss or perlite. A well-drained medium is critical. Water well while growing and give a brief winter rest of two to three weeks. Never allow the plants to dry out completely. Light shade with good air movement and humidity are also needed.

Classification

Maxillaria lepidota Lindley 1845.

Maxillaria lepidota

Maxillaria picta

Found in southeastern Brazil and Argentina, this is an epiphytic orchid (occasionally lithophytic) with ovoid ribbed pseudobulbs that are either spaced apart or clustered along a creeping rhizome. The leaves are up to 12 inches (30 cm) long and up to 2 inches (5 cm) wide, erect or spreading, ligulate and acute. There are many single flowered inflorescences on each plant. The flowers are golden yellow inside; outside they are creamy yellow with purplish brown flecks. The three-lobed lip is erect and spreading. It is white, yellow, or cream in color with a red-spotted base. The midlobe has undulate margins. The column is erect and slightly incurved.

Cultivation

Grow at intermediate temperatures in pots containing fine bark with small amounts of sphagnum moss or perlite. A well-drained medium is critical. Water well while growing and give a brief winter rest of two to three weeks. Never allow the plants to dry out completely. Light shade with good air movement and humidity are also needed.

Classification

Maxillaria picta Hooker 1832.

Maxillaria picta

Maxillaria striata

This epiphytic pseudbulbous orchid grows in very wet montane forests at elevations of up to 4,500 feet (1,400 m) in the Andes of Peru, Ecuador, and Colombia. The pseudobulbs are ovoid to oblong or cylindrical, with several pairs of sheaths and a single leaf at the apex. The leathery oblong to elliptical leaf is up to 9 inches (23 cm) long. The inflorescence emerges laterally from the base of mature pseudobulbs and has one showy flower, up to 5 inches (13 cm) across. Flower color varies from yellowish to pale reddish brown with brown longitudinal stripes. The three-lobed lip is white with red veins. The column is short, stout, and club shaped.

Cultivation

Grow at intermediate temperatures in pots containing fine bark with a little sphagnum moss or perlite. A well-drained medium is critical. Water well while growing and give a brief winter rest of two to three weeks. Never allow the plants to dry out completely. Light shade with good air movement and humidity are also needed.

Classification

Maxillaria striata Rolfe 1893.

Maxillaria striata

Other *Maxillaria* Species

Above: *Maxillaria friedrichstalii* from southeast Mexico to Panama.

Left: *Maxillaria praestans* from Central America.

Above: *Maxillaria acuminata* from Colombia, Ecuador, and Peru.

Right: *Maxillaria setigera* from Guyana, Venezuela, Colombia, Ecuador, Peru, and Brazil.

Left: *Maxillaria longipes* from Ecuador to Peru.

Miltonia

DATA

Number of Species: About 20.

Classification: *Miltonia* Lindley 1837; tribe Cymbidieae, subtribe Oncidiinae.

Form: Epiphytic herbs with inconspicuous compressed pseudobulbs bearing one or two apical leaves, with base enveloped in foliaceous sheaths. Leaves are linear to elliptical, pale to dark green. Inflorescence is axillary, erect, or arching, with one to many flowers. Flowers are showy, widely spreading, small to large in size on long pedicels. The petals are often slightly wider than the sepals, making the flower appear flat. The lip is broadly spreading, entire, with a shortly clawed or sessile base; the disc is inconspicuous or lamellate. The column is short, lacking a foot, and bears two ovoid, waxy pollinia.

Distribution: Brazil, Peru.

Habitat: Humid and wet forest at elevations of 2,400 to 3,000 ft (700–900 m).

These orchids are named for Earl Fitzwilliam, Viscount Milton (1786–1857), a keen orchid grower, from the north of England. *Miltonia* are commonly referred to as the "pansy orchids," as are members of the genus *Miltoniopsis*. *Miltonia spectabilis* is the type species as described by John Lindley in 1837 and is considered the most pansylike. Numerous natural *Miltonia* hybrids occur, and *Miltonia* contributes to numerous cultivated intergeneric hybrids.

Cultivation

Many enthusiasts find these orchids tricky to grow, but the key is to keep them moist. Grow them in pots, baskets, and pans. Mix peat substitute or leaf mold and sphagnum moss together with added bark to form a free-draining medium. Water the plants liberally every seven to 10 days, soaking the compost thoroughly. Allow them to dry almost completely before rewatering, but always keep the surroundings moist by standing the container on a tray of damp pebbles.

Feed only a weak fertilizer once every two to three weeks. Good bright light is important, but shade the plants from direct sunlight. Leaves should be light green; if a darkening of the leaves is noticed, light levels should be increased. Mist the plants only on hot dry days, preferably in the early morning, but never leave water on the leaves. Avoid misting of the flowers since this causes unsightly spots. Maintain a nighttime temperature of 55°F (13°C) and a daytime temperature of 75°F (24°C).

Miltonia x *bluntii* is a natural hybrid between *M. clowesii* and *M. spectabilis* from southeastern Brazil.

Miltonia cuneata

This orchid grows in Brazil in the states of Espírito Santo, Rio de Janeiro, and São Paulo and is known at elevations from 2,600 to 3,300 feet (800–1,000 m) in dense hillside forests. The pseudobulbs range from clustered to well spaced, ovate to oblong, and are compressed and slightly tapering. There are two to three ligulate and oblong leaves, keeled on the underside and measure 9 to 15 inches (23–38 cm) long.

The inflorescence is racemose, 12 to 24 inches (30–60 cm) long and bears six to eight flowers. The flowers themselves are 2.5 to 4 inches (6.5–10.5 cm) across. The sepals and petals are a deep chestnut brown with yellowish green tips. The apex of the lip is white and the wedge-shaped base has two keels that may be spotted with rose or purple.

Cultivation

The requirements of this species are typical for the genus. Grow in pots, baskets, and pans. Mix peat substitute or leaf mold and sphagnum moss together with added bark to form a free-draining medium. Water liberally every seven to 10 days, soaking the compost and allow it to almost dry completely before rewatering. Always keep the surroundings moist by standing the container on a tray of damp pebbles. Feed only a weak fertilizer once every two to three weeks. Good bright light is important, but shade the growing plants from direct sunlight. Leaves should be light green; if a darkening of the leaves is noticed, then light levels should be increased. Mist the plants only on hot dry days, preferably in the early morning, but never leave water on the leaves. Avoid misting of the flowers since this will cause unsightly spots. Maintain a nighttime temperature of 55°F (13°C) and a daytime temperature of 75°F (24°C).

Classification

Miltonia cuneata Lindley 1844.

Miltonia cuneata

Miltonia moreliana

Occurring over a wide area of south-central Brazil, this is *Miltonia moreliana*. *Miltonia spectabilis* var. *moreliana*—the name which was used until recently—was first grown and flowered in France by a Monsieur Morel. Like most of the orchids described in the 19th century, little was made known concerning its location and habitat for fear that rival collectors would gain access to the area.

The pseudobulbs are ovoid to oblong, glossy greenish yellow, and closely spaced along the creeping rhizome. The two leaves are linear ligulate and 4 to 7 inches (10–17.5 cm) long. The inflorescence is erect, 10 inches (25 cm) long, and sheathed with flattened bracts. The flowers are single and measure 4 inches (10 cm) in diameter. They have white sepals and petals, flushed with pale rose down the center. The lip is a bright rose red color with distinct veins of rose or purple.

Cultivation

Miltonia moreliana can be best grown in a basket using a peat substitute or leaf mold and moss mix with a little bark for food drainage. Soak every seven to 10 days in a bucket of water, then allow to drain. The plant must always be kept moist, so the compost may need misting on hot days—never allow it to dry out. Good bright light is important, but shade the plant from direct sunlight. Feed it only a weak fertilizer.

Good air circulation is essential, and a nighttime temperature of 55°F (13°C), increasing to 75°F (24°C) during the day, should be maintained. Cultivated plants bloom in late spring or summer.

Classification

Miltonia moreliana A. Richard 1848.

Miltonia moreliana

Miltonia Hybrids

Miltonia Soquel 'Volcano Snow'

Miltonia 'Andy Easton'

Miltonia 'Hannover Fire'

Miltonia 'Honolulu'

Miltonia Many Waters 'Goshawk'

Odontoglossum

DATA

Number of Species: About 60.

Classification: *Odontoglossum*
H. B. K. 1815 A. von Humboldt,
A. Bonpland. C. S. Kuntz; tribe
Cymbidieae, subtribe Oncidiinae.

Form: Medium to large plants
with a short creeping rhizome.
Pseudobulbs are compressed,
ovoid, elliptical–oblong, with one
to three leaves at the apex and
distichous leaf-bearing sheaths
at the base. Leaves are rigid or
flexible, leathery or fleshy.
Numerous flowers, usually large
and showy, sometimes small and
insignificant; may be red, purple,
brown, yellow, or white. Lip is
entire to three-lobed; side lobes
are spreading or erect; midlobes
deflexed. Column is slender and
long, with two waxy pollinia.

Distribution: Central and
subtropical South America.

Habitat: Grow as epiphytes or
lithophytes in mountainous
rainforest regions with high
humidity.

The name *Odontoglossum* comes from the Greek *odonto*, meaning
"tooth"—a reference to the toothlike projections on the lip—and
glossa, meaning "tongue." These orchids grow at altitudes of 4,200 to
10,500 feet (1,300– 3,200 m) in cool but humid conditions with good
dappled light to shade. There are two distinct groups and six subgenera.
The six subgenera are *Erectolobata*, *Lindleyana*, *Nevadensia*,
Odontoglossum, *Serratolaminata*, and *Unguisepala*. Within four of the
subgenera the inflorescence grows to a short length and bears up to 20
flowers; in the other two genera the inflorescence is long and arching
and can bear, depending on species, up to 150 flowers.

John Lindley undertook the first revision of the genus in 1852 in
Flora Orchidacea. Over the years species have been included and then
excluded from the genus. The use of DNA analysis has proved invaluable
in this exercise.

Numerous natural hybrids occur between species in the genus.
More significantly, *Odontoglossum* lends itself to the production of many
artificial intergeneric hybrids. The hybrids with red pigmentation nearly
all derive from a crossing with the genus *Cochlioda*, especially with
Cochlioda noezliana. A sample of intergeneric hybrids is given overleaf.

Cultivation

Pot-grown orchids should be raised in a mix of equal quantities bark,
peat substitute or leaf mold, perlite, and coarse sand. When choosing a
pot, use one size smaller than you normally would, since these orchids
like to be tight in the pot. Provide good light but avoid direct sunlight,

Odontoglossum crispum is a cool-growing species from Colombia.

and ensure that there is shade in the summer. Temperature should be about 50 to 54°F (10-12°C) in winter and 68 to 75°F (20 to 24°C) in summer while the plant is growing. A good air flow and constant humidity of 70 to 80 percent are essential. Keep the plants moist; they should not be drenched nor allowed to dry out. Use a balanced fertilizer mixed at 25 percent of normal strength. During the winter follow the routine of watering three times, feeding once, followed by three more waterings. During the summer plants should be given three feeds then flushed with clean water to remove undissolved salts.

Repotting can be done every two years (using the smallest possible pot size). Newly potted plants should be sprayed and placed in shade until new growth is seen, after which the normal watering regime can be continued.

Odontoglossum multistellare is from Peru.

Examples of Intergeneric Hybrids with *Odontoglossum*

Cochlioda x *Miltonia* x *Odontoglossum* x *Oncidium* = x *Burrageara*

Brassia x *Odontoglossum* x *Oncidium* = x *Maclellanara*

Odontoglossum x *Cochlioda* = x *Odontioda*

Brassia x *Odontoglossum* = x *Odontobrassia*

Odontoglossum x *Oncidium* = x *Odontocidium*

Miltonia x *Odontoglossum* = x *Odontonia*

Cochlioda x *Miltonia* x *Odontoglossum* = x *Vuylstekeara*

Cochlioda x *Odontoglossum* x *Oncidium* = x *Wilsonara*

Odontoglossum aspidorhinum

An epiphyte growing at an altitude of 4,500 to 7,500 feet (1,400-2,300 m), *Odontoglossum aspidorhinum* occurs in Colombia and northern Equador. Its pseudobulbs are ovate, narrowing to the apex, and bear two linear leaves. The inflorescence is 8 inches (20 cm) long and erect, with up to 15 widely spaced flowers. Petals and sepals are yellow with reddish brown markings and the lip is white with pink markings near the base. The column is yellow.

Cultivation

Pot into the smallest pot for the size of the plant, using equal parts of coarse sand, bark, perlite, and peat substitute or leaf mold. Never allow the compost to dry out, and maintain constant humidity. When actively growing in the summer, the plant should be given balanced fertilizer at one-quarter strength, flushed out with plain water after every three feeds. During the winter months when there is less light, change the regime to three weeks of watering followed by one week of feeding.

The plants thrive on good bright light (but not direct sunlight), and should be shaded 50 percent during summer. Keep the temperature in winter at 50 to 54°F (10-12°C) and in summer at 68 to 75°F (20-24°C). In summer the plants benefit from a nighttime drop in temperature of 11 to 14°F (6-8°C), which can be achieved by leaving the greenhouse door open during the night. Ensure all windows and doors are closed during the day. Repot every two years, or as the compost breaks down, into the smallest possible pot.

Classification

Odontoglossum aspidorhynum F. Lehmann 1895.

Odontoglossum aspidorhinum

Odontoglossum astranthum

This epiphytic orchid from Equador and Peru produces a branching panicle bearing upwards of 50 flowers. Flowers are 2 inches (5 cm) in diameter. The sepals and petals are lanceolate and acuminate, yellowish with purple or brown blotches and streaks. The lip is ligulate, pointed in front, and white with pale rose-colored dots. The column base is orange with reddish or purple spots.

Cultivation

Pot into the smallest pot for the size of the plant, using equal parts of coarse sand, bark, perlite, and peat substitute or leaf mold. Never allow the compost to dry out, and maintain constant humidity. When actively growing in the summer, the plant should be given balanced fertilizer at one-quarter strength, flushed out with plain water after every three feeds. During the winter months when there is less light, change the regime to three weeks of watering followed by one week of feeding.

The plants thrive on good bright light (but not direct sunlight), and should be shaded 50 percent during summer. Keep the temperature in winter at 50 to 54°F (10–12°C) and in summer at 68 to 75°F (20–24°C). In summer the plants benefit from a nighttime drop in temperature of 11 to 14°F (6–8°C), which can be achieved by leaving the greenhouse door open during the night. Ensure all windows and doors are closed during the day. Repot every two years, or as the compost breaks down, into the smallest possible pot.

Classification

Odontoglossum astranthum Linden, Reichenbach f. 1887.

Odontoglossum astranthum

Odontoglossum crocidipterum

Known as the Saffron Yellow Two-winged Odontoglossum, *Odontoglossum crocidipterum* is an epiphytic orchid from wet mountain forests of Colombia and Venezuela. Its pseudobulbs are ovoid to elliptical, tapering to the apex, and frequently spotted purple. Leaves are oblong to linear lanceolate, 10 inches long by 1.5 inches across (25 by 4 cm). It blooms in winter on an ascending or arching 8-inch- (20-cm-) long racemose or paniculate inflorescence, with fragrant small flowers arising on a newly maturing pseudobulb. Petals and sepals are white or pale yellow to yellow brown with spots of dark chocolate brown. The lip has a large brown spot on the anterior part, with a smaller one on each side of white calluses. The column is 0.5 inch (13 mm) long with narrow wings.

Cultivation

Pot into the smallest pot for the size of the plant, using equal parts of coarse sand, bark, perlite, and peat substitute or leaf mold. Never allow the compost to dry out, and maintain constant humidity. When actively growing in the summer, the plant should be given balanced fertilizer at one-quarter strength, flushed out with plain water after every three feeds. During the winter months when there is less light, change the regime to three weeks of watering followed by one week of feeding.

The plants thrive on good bright light (not direct sunlight), and should be half shaded during summer. Keep winter temperatures in the range of 50 to 54°F (10–12°C). In summer temperatures should be around 68 to 75°F with a nighttime drop of 11 to 14°F (6–8°C), which can be achieved by leaving the greenhouse door open during the night. Ensure all windows and doors are closed during the day. Repot every two years, or as the compost breaks down, into the smallest possible pot.

Classification

Odontoglossum crocidipterum Reichenbach.f. 1871.

Odontoglossum crocidipterum

Odontoglossum harryanum

Found in montane forests at 5,400 to 6,900 feet (1,600–2,100 m), *Odontoglossum harryanum* is an epiphyte from Colombia. The pseudobulbs are clustered together; each one is up to 4 inches (10 cm) tall, oblong, ovate, compressed, and smooth when young but becoming furrowed with age. There are two leathery leaves 6 to 12 inches (15 to 30 cm) long. The racemose suberect inflorescence reaches up to 39 inches (1 m) in length and bears 6 to 12 flowers. Flowers are 3 to 5 inches (7.5 to 13 cm) in diameter with yellow sepals and petals marked with pale chestnut brown; petals are purple lined at the base. The lip is three-lobed, oblong-oval, with up-curving lateral lobes, white heavily streaked with feathery lines of bluish purple; the anterior lobes are white, changing to yellow and the crest has a fringed, deep yellow margin.

Cultivation

Pot into the smallest pot for the size of the plant, using equal parts of coarse sand, bark, perlite, and peat substitute or leaf mold. Never allow the compost to dry out, and maintain constant humidity. When actively growing in the summer, the plant should be given balanced fertilizer at one-quarter strength, flushed out with plain water after every three feeds. During winter when there is less light, change to three weeks of watering followed by one week of feeding.

The plants thrive on good bright light (not direct sunlight), and should be half shaded in summer. Keep winter temperatures at about 50 to 54°F (10–12°C). Temperatures in summer should be from 68 to 75°F with a nighttime drop of 11 to 14°F (6–8°C), which can be achieved by leaving the greenhouse door open. All windows and doors must be closed during the day. Repot every two years, or as the compost breaks down, into the smallest possible pot.

Classification

Odontoglossum harryanum Reichenbach f. 1886.

Odontoglossum harryanum

Hybrids Involving *Odontoglossum*

x *Burrageara* 'Stefan Isler'

x *Burrageara* 'Nelly Isler'

Odontoglossum 'Cathay'

x *Maclellanara* 'Pagan Lovesong No. 1'

x *Odontobrassia* 'Billabong'

x *Odontioda* 'Joe's Drum'

x *Vuylstekeara* Cambria 'Plush'

363

x *Wilsonara* 'Tiger Talk Beacon'

x *Wilsonara* 'Ravissement La Réunion'

Oncidium

DATA

Number of Species: Over 600.

Classification: *Oncidium*
Schwartz, O. 1800; tribe
Cymbidieae, subtribe Oncidiinae

Form: Rhizome creeping in long
and short forms. Pseudobulbs
vary in size and shape. One to
four leaves, flat or terete, leathery
or soft. In softer-leaved species a
pair of basal leaves sheath the
pseudobulbs. Inflorescence basal,
racemose to paniculate, arching,
branching, and pendent, bearing
few to many flowers. Sepals
subsimilar, spreading or relaxed.
Petals similar to dorsal sepal but
larger. Lip at right angles to
column, entire to three-lobed,
side lobes spreading forward or
downward. Column short, stout,
erect, with a fleshy plate below
the stigma. Pollinia two, waxy.

Distribution: Tropical to
subtropical America.

Habitat: To 13,300 ft (4,000 m).
Mainly epiphytes; some
lithophytes and terrestrial species.

The name *Oncidium* is derived from the Greek *onkus*, meaning "mass"
or "pad," which refers to the fleshy warty callus on the lip of many
members of the genus. Many of the original species have been moved
to similar genera such as *Odontoglossum*, *Brassia*, or *Miltonia*, but
Oncidium remains a very large genus in its own right. Flowers within
the genus range from the inconspicuous to the large—up to 5 inches
(13 cm) in diameter—and are mostly yellow or brown in color.

Cultivation

Since it is one of the larger genera with members occupying a wide
range of habitats, there is no one method of cultivation that will suit
all *Oncidium* species. Growing as they do from sea level to the higher
reaches of the Andes mountain range, it makes the recommendation of
cultural methods very difficult. If buying a new plant, ask at the initial
point of sale how its needs should be met. Alternatively, when it needs
to be repotted seek advice either by word of mouth, from books, or on
the Internet. The following should be used only as a guide:

Containers. Different-sized plants can be grown successfully in pots,
pans, baskets, and on slabs. For pans and pots use a fine to medium
bark. For species with large pseudobulbs use pots or baskets containing
a medium of six parts bark, one part coarse peat substitute or leaf mold,
one part pumice, and one part charcoal. On slabs, gently wrap damp
sphagnum moss around the roots before tying to the slab. Smaller
pseudobulbs can be affixed in the same manner to bark rafts.

Oncidium divaricatum (pulvinatum) is from southern
Brazil and northeastern Argentina.

Temperature. Because of the variety of different habitats there is no set temperature. Nighttime temperature should be intermediate to warm—55 to 60°F (12.8–15.6°C). Daytime temperature can be allowed to rise to 80 to 85°F (26.7–29.4°C). If you are unable to maintain a good humid atmosphere, the plants will tolerate temperatures up to 95°F (35°C). With the rise in temperature and humidity there must be good air circulation, or the plants will suffer.

Watering. Great care is needed, since the amount of water required will vary according to species. The thin-leaved or thin-rooted plants need to have a lot more water than those with thick leaves and roots. Water well while the plant is in active growth. Many plants take a winter rest and will therefore only require to be kept damp in order to prevent the pseudobulbs from shriveling.

Humidity. If grown on a tray of stones or pebbles, put enough water in the tray to come just below the base of the pot. The humidity created by this method in a greenhouse will be sufficient. The same applies for plants grown indoors. The required humidity levels of 30 to 65 percent are not as high as for some other orchids.

Light. The quantity and quality of light needed will depend on the species. Those referred to as "mule-eared" because of their thicker leaves will have the ability to withstand more light. Within the genus there are those that can take some direct sunlight for short periods, but in general a well-lit shaded area is recommended.

Oncidium concolor is from southern Brazil and northeastern Argentina.

Fertilizer. Apply a liquid fertilizer every two to four weeks during the growing season. Flush with clear water after every third fertilizing session to remove any salt buildup. During cloudy months once a month will be sufficient.

Potting. Always pot the newest growth toward the center of a pot to allow room for further new growths. For plants with small pseudobulbs use a fine bark mix; larger species will need a medium bark mix. Pot on in the spring and give the plant time to stabilize and make new growths. Keep it dry until new root is observed then begin to add water to the pot. Good humidity while waiting for root growth will keep the plant going.

A plant grown in free-draining medium and provided with good humidity, light, and air movement will reward you with blooms.

Intergeneric Hybrids

Many hybrids have been bred mainly with *Odontoglossum*, *Miltonia*, and *Brassia* species. Examples are:

Aspasia x *Miltonia* x *Odontoglossum* x *Oncidium* = x *Withnerara*
Brassia x *Oncidium* = x *Brassidium*
Cochlioda x *Miltonia* x *Odontoglossum* x *Oncidium* = x *Burrageara*
Cochlioda x *Odontoglossum* x *Oncidium* = x *Wilsonara*
Miltonia x *Odontoglossum* x *Oncidium* = x *Colmanara*
Odontoglossum x *Oncidium* = x *Odontocidium*

Oncidium cavendishianum

Previously known as *Trichocentrum cavendishianum*, this is an epiphytic orchid found at heights up to 9,200 feet (2,800 m) in Mexico, Honduras, and Guatemala. The pseudobulbs are 0.75 inch (20 mm) long and wrapped in a distichous, dried-up sheath. The erect leaves are elliptical or lanceolate. They measure 6 to 18 inches (15–45 cm) long and are yellowish or green. The inflorescence is erect, stout, 24 to 54 inches (60–150 cm) in length, and multiflowered. The flowers are fragrant, showy, and waxy. The sepals and petals are yellowish green or yellow blotched with red or brown. The lip is deep yellow, while the trilobed callus is white, dotted with red or brown. The column is 0.4 inch (1 cm) long, stout, with yellow wings dotted with red.

Cultivation

This plant should be grown epiphytically on bark or in baskets with good drainage. It requires full light, high humidity, regular misting in summer, and intermediate growing conditions. Water it well during the growing period, but less in the resting period. Flowering occurs during winter and spring.

Classification

Oncidium cavendishianum Bateman 1837.

Oncidium cavendishianum

Oncidium hastilabium

First described as *Odontoglossum hastilabium* by John Lindley in 1846, this orchid was transferred to the genus *Oncidium* by L. Garay and G. S. K. Dunsterville in 1976. *Oncidium hastilabium* is a creeping epiphyte of moderate elevations in the Andes, from Colombia and Venezuela to Peru. The pseudobulbs are clustered and compressed, oblong to ovoid in shape, and measuring 2.5 inches by 1.5 inches (6 x 4 cm). Leaves are lanceolate and obtuse or mucronate at the apex. They are 14 inches long and 1.5 inches across (35 x 4 cm).

The arching inflorescence is up to 30 inches (75 cm) in length and multiflowered. The fragrant flowers open in succession and are longlived. Petals and sepals are pale yellow or green, with horizontal chocolate brown stripes. The white lip has a purple or rose base and is trilobed, the lateral lobes being small, while the midlobe is clawed. The callus is three-keeled. The column is lavender or purple with a yellow base.

Cultivation

Oncidium hastilabium has no special cultivation requirements and grows best in pots using an epiphytic substrate, in sun or partial shade. Water regularly but avoid overwatering. It is best grown in cool to intermediate conditions.

Classification

Oncidium hastilabium Lindley 1854.

Oncidium hastilabium

Oncidium ornithorhynchum

This species grows as an epiphyte in moist forests from Mexico to Colombia at altitudes of 3,900 to 5,900 feet (1,200–1,800 m). Pseudobulbs are ovoid to oblong with two leaves at the apex. The leaves are 30 inches (17 cm) long and 1.5 inches (4 cm) wide, oblong to oblanceolate in shape, and pale green or gray green in color. The arching multiflowered inflorescence is up to 20 inches (50 cm) long. Flowers are 1 inch (2.5 cm) across. The petals and sepals are pink, purple, or white, with a golden yellow to deep orange callus. The lip is darker than the petals and sepals, shortly clawed, and three-lobed to hastate. The column is erect, 0.2 inches (5 mm) long; wings are broadly triangular and the anther is beak shaped.

Cultivation

This fragrant floriferous plant often produces four or five branched inflorescences per pseudobulb. Ideally suited to pot culture, it requires even moisture all year round, with high humidity, some shade, good air movement, and cool to intermediate temperatures.

Classification

Oncidium ornithorhynchum H. B. K. 1816. First described by F. H. A. von Humboldt, A. Bonpland, and C. S. Kuntz in 1815.

Oncidium ornithorhynchum

Other *Oncidium* Species

Oncidium forbesii from southeastern Brazil.

Oncidium sarcodes from southeastern and southern Brazil.

Oncidium chrysomorphum from Venezuela to Ecuador.

Ophrys

Number of Species: About 252.

Classification: *Ophrys* Linnaeus 1753; tribe Orchideae, subtribe Orchidinae.

Form: Terrestrial herbs, with two ovoid or elliptical tubers or root stem tuberoids. Leaves form a basal rosette. Form of flowers mimics bees or other insects. The sepals are spreading; the smaller petals are elongated and antennalike, sometimes with a wavy edge. The lip points downward, is entire or lobed, lacks a spur, and has short hairs to the margins. The central speculum is defined as H, W, or X shaped, or as an omega sign or even a solid blotch. Flower colors range from blue through steely blue to gray. Inflorescence erect and bears two or more flowers.

Distribution: Europe, western Asia, North Africa.

Habitat: Full sun or semishade on alkaline to slightly acid, dry, cool soil, in scrubland, open woodland, garigue, fields, and olive groves.

The name for this genus comes from the Greek for "eyebrow"; the leaves may have been used in the past to dye eyebrows or hair. *Ophrys* species are often known as bee orchids because of their form, which mimics that of a bee. Individual species mimic the shape or fragrance (pheromones) that particular insect species use to attract a male suitor, which attempts to copulate (pseudocopulate) with the flower. In the process pollinia become attached to the head of the pollinator, and the pollen is then transferred to the next flower the insect attempts to mate with. Bees and wasps are the main pollinators.

Cultivation

It is critical that specimens are obtained from a reputable source and not taken directly from the wild.

Ophrys can be grown in free-draining pots in an alpine house. A garden soil rich in humus with added peat substitute or leaf mold that remains damp is suitable. Calcareous soil and sand have also proved successful. Most species prefer an alkaline-based medium, while a few tend toward slightly acidic media. During the growing season provide a good supply of water. Once the flowers and leaves have disappeared, however, simply keep the tubers slightly damp during this rest period. Only start to give water when new growth appears. A weak fertilizer may be given during the growth period. Handle all tubers with care, since they do not like to be disturbed.

The highly variable *Ophrys holoserica* grows in scrub and grassland throughout much of western and central Europe as far as the Mediterranean.

Orchis

DATA

Number of Species: About 60.

Classification: *Orchis* Linnaeus 1753; tribe Orchideae, subtribe Orchidinae.

Form: Tuberous rooted with two or three tubers and no pseudobulbs. Root stem tuberoids are ovoid or ellipsoid. Leaves linear-lanceolate to oblong-ovate, forming a basal rosette. Inflorescences are erect, laxly to densely multiflowered. Flowers are showy pink, purple, red, or white. Petals are of equal size and sepals are incurved forming a hood; lateral sepals are spreading and deflexed. The lip is entire or three-lobed, extending forward or decurved: the spur is slender or saccate, the ovary cylindrical, and the column erect with a three-lobed rostellum.

Distribution: Northern Europe, Mediterranean, east to China.

Habitat: Nearly all terrestrial on alkaline to acidic damp soils on short grassland, open garigue, wooded areas, and scrubland, often with calcareous substrates.

The shape of the tuberous roots gives this genus its name—*Orchis* is derived from the Greek word meaning "testicle" and was first used in 1753 to describe these plants by Carolus Linnaeus (Carl von Linné). In earlier times the resemblance of the roots to body parts led people to believe that *Orchis* had medicinal properties, in particular the ability to increase fertility. In Turkey, the drink *salep* is made from orchid tubers, which has led to the overcollecting of wild populations.

Cultivation

Before attempting to grow *Orchis* species make sure that they are from a nursery-propagated source and not from the wild.

Orchis can be pot-grown but they do better in a raised bed. Fill the bed with good garden loam with added peat substitute and leaf mold, dug in to a depth of 18 inches (45 cm). The soil must be porous enough to drain but still remain moist. *Orchis* species can be divided into two groups: those that like acidic soil and those that prefer alkaline soil. It is possible to split the bed into two halves with different soil pH. Calcareous soil lovers benefit from the addition of limestone or chalk. Rhizomes or tuberous roots are best planted in the fall. Check species requirements for sunlight and shade. After flowering, the plants need a rest period.If you are planting in pots, you will need a well-drained medium and a good depth of pot. Protect them from frost—an alpine house is ideal. Handle rhizome or tuberous roots carefully. Keep them moist during the winter and increase water as new growth appears. A weak fertilizer may be given.

Orchis sancta (Anacamptis sancta) is from the eastern Mediterranean to the Caucasus.

Orchis mascula

This species, found over much of western and central Europe, flowers in spring and is known as the Early Purple Orchid. It has two ovoid tubers and erect reddish brown stems which are 8 to 24 inches tall (20–60 cm). Four to eight basal leaves form a rosette or grow near erect, and they may be unmarked or have violet or brown blotches. There are also two to four cauline leaves. The bracts are membranous and flushed violet. Between six and 20 flowers are borne on the dense inflorescence; they range in color from crimson red to purplish, and very occasionally pink or white. The dorsal sepal is near erect or forms a hood with the petals, while the three-lobed lip is slightly convex to sharply folded longitudinally. The base is yellow or white with a velvety texture, and the spur is horizontal or vertical.

Cultivation

Pot-grown orchids require a sowing medium that can be well drained yet retain moisture, such as a rich humus-based soil with added peat substitute. A good depth of pot is essential to accommodate roots and maximize moisture retention. Alpine houses are ideal for keeping the growing plants frost free. Once flowering is over and the leaves have died away, a rest period must be given. The pot should be kept damp until new shoots appear, at which stage watering may be increased. Feed with a weak liquid fertilizer. Outside beds are probably best at this stage, since the tuber can be set deep and kept frost free. Cold to cool temperatures are preferred.

Classification

Orchis mascula (L.) Linnaeus 1755.

Orchis mascula

Paphiopedilum

DATA

Number of species: About 100.

Classification: *Paphiopedilum* Pfitzer 1886; tribe Cypripedieae, subtribe Paphiopedilinae.

Form: Typically fanshaped, with thick roots spreading from the base. Pseudobulbs absent. Leaves light green on top with purple hue beneath. The tubular inflorescence is terminal, stiff, and hairy, with one or more green, brown, yellow, or white waxy flowers. There is a large dorsal erect sepal, which is sometimes cowl-like, with fused lateral sepals. Petals horizontal, covered in bumps and hairs. The lip is pouch shaped. Column is short with a fleshy staminode at its apex. Behind the staminode is a short stalk bearing the stigmatic surface, between two fertile anthers bearing two pollinia.

Distribution: China to the Himalayas to Southeast Asia.

Habitat: Terrestrial, occasionally lithophytic or epiphytic.

Members of this genus are commonly known as lady's slipper orchids, a broad translation of the Greek *Paphiopedilum,* from the words Paphos (a temple city on Cyprus dedicated to Aphrodite) and *pedilum* ("slipper"). Most species grow at moderate altitudes under dense shade on the forest floor, but some are found on rock faces. They are notoriously difficult to grow from seed, and collection of plants from the wild has put great pressure on native populations as a result. Active conservation measures are in place to conserve some species in the wild.

There are more hybrid paphiopedilums than any other orchid genus—many thousands are registered. The trend is to develop vigorous plants with large colorful flowers that bloom several times a year.

Cultivation

These orchids grow naturally on the ground, rooted in leaf mold. In greenhouse conditions they grow best in pots containing six parts bark, one part perlag or pumice, one part charcoal, and one part coarse peat substitute. The medium must be well drained yet hold a little moisture. Humidity is crucial—the plants must be kept damp without becoming soaking wet. Single plants can stand on a gravel tray, but do not allow the water to touch the base. Air movement and shade are required, but too much shade can lead to leaf growth rather than flower production.

Individual species come from cool to warm habitats, so check the appropriate temperature range for each species. For example, *Paphiopedilum amabile* likes warm conditions while *P. venustum* requires cool to intermediate conditions. Minimum winter temperature is 65 to 75°F (15–18°C). Feed regularly with a weak liquid fertilizer.

The highly popular white-flowered *Paphiopedilum niveum.*

Paphiopedilum delanatii

This is a terrestrial and lithophytic species from Vietnam, growing at an elevation of 2,250 to 4,500 feet (690–1,400 m). It usually grows in moss cracks and crevasses mostly facing east or south, where the soils are rich in silicates or are acidic. In the wild it receives little water from January to May, with heavy rainfall from June to December.

Paphiopedilum delanatii is a spring-flowering orchid that prefers a warm environment. It has five to seven narrowly elliptical leaves on a plant, arranged in two rows. Leaves are mottled dark green to light green on top and spotted purple on the underside. The inflorescence is erect with a pubescent reddish flowering stem, 8 to 9 inches (20–22.5 cm) tall. The inflorescence bears one or two flowers, which are pale pink with red or yellow markings on the staminode.

Cultivation

This orchid is best grown in pots containing a free-draining moist compost, made up of 80 percent bark and 20 percent coarse peat substitute, to which may be added small amounts of charcoal and perlag. Water well once a week during June to December and withdraw water from January to May, but keep the compost moist and never allow it to dry out completely. Give good but shaded light. *Paphiopedilum delanatii* requires good air movement and good humidity—standing the pot on a tray of wet pebbles will increase the humidity. Apply a balanced weak fertilizer weekly throughout the year. The minimum temperature required is 60 to 65°F (15–18°C). Repot when the compost has broken down or at least every two years.

Classification

Paphiopedilum delanatii Guillaumin 1924.

Paphiopedilum delanatii

Paphiopedilum gratrixianum

This terrestrial lithophytic orchid is found in North Vietnam and Southeast Asia, where it grows in leaf litter in wet cloud forest conditions at elevations of 2,100 to 3,600 feet (640–1,100 m). It has four to seven suberect leaves, which are green with purple spotting on the underside.

The flowering stem is 10 inches (25 cm) tall and bears a single flower. The dorsal sepal is pubescent, pale green at the base, spotted with purple, and white above. The petals are shiny, flushed brown with a yellow lip, and veined with reddish brown.

Cultivation

Grow *Paphiopedilum gratrixianum* in pots containing 80 percent bark and 20 percent coarse peat substitute. The addition of perlag, charcoal, and perlite can be beneficial. The medium must be free-draining but able to hold moisture. Do not allow it to dry out. Water well once a week, drain, and stand the pot on a tray of pebbles. This plant requires good air flow and humid conditions. Give good but shaded light. Feed weekly with a weak balanced fertilizer. A well-grown plant will produce flowers up to 3 inches (8 cm) in size.

Classification

Paphiopedilum gratrixianum Guillaumin 1924.

Paphiopedilum gratrixianum

Paphiopedilum henryanum

This orchid occurs in China and North Vietnam at elevations of 1,800 to 4,200 feet (550–1,300 m). It is a small compact lithophyte found mostly in mixed tree and conifer forests, but also on steep limestone cliffs and hillsides. The three distichous leaves are sharply keeled at the base, glossy dark green in color on the topside, with a paler green underside.

The single flower is terminal on a 3-inch- (7.5-cm-) tall flowering stem. The flower lip is intensely purple or red in color with a metallic gloss or sheen. The upper dorsal sepal is broad, yellow or green in color, and covered with red or brown spots of differing sizes. The lateral sepals are undulate and also have red or brown spotting. Flower size varies from 1.5 to 2.5 inches (4–6 cm).

Cultivation

Cultivate *Paphiopedilum henryanum* in pots containing a well-drained medium of 80 percent bark with 20 percent coarse peat substitute. Additives such as perlag, perlite, and charcoal may be used. Water all year round but do not stand the pot in water. This plants likes high humidity, so place the pot on a tray of damp pebbles and maintain good air flow. It requires good but shaded light and should never be exposed to direct sunlight. Grow in cool to intermediate conditions and feed weekly with a weak balanced fertilizer.

Classification

Paphiopedilum henryanum Braemin 1987.

Paphiopedilum henryanum

Paphiopedilum insigne

An epiphytic orchid that grows on rocks exposed to monsoon rains, *Paphiopedilum insigne* occurs in India and Nepal at elevations of 3,000 to 6,000 feet (900–1,800 m). The strap-shaped leaves measure 8 to 12 inches (20–30 cm) long and 1 inch (2.5 cm) across.

A single terminal flower is borne on a dark green or brown scape that has a reddish pubescence and bears an ovate bract. The flower is 4 to 5 inches (10–13 cm) across and has a glossy, or varnished, appearance. The dorsal sepal is broadly ovate, green with white margins, and spotted brown. The synsepalum is pale green with smaller brown spotting. The petals are yellowish green with pale brown veining. The lip is a golden or brown color with darker brown veining. This species is widely used in hybridizing.

Cultivation

Grow this vigorous orchid in pots containing a water-retentive medium of 80 percent bark with 20 percent coarse peat substitute. The addition of charcoal and perlag will ensure draining and help hold moisture. Change the compost every two years, or earlier if necessary. *Paphiopedilum insigne* does not require a rest period and can have water all year, although the amount should be reduced when the plant is not in flower. It requires good air flow, humidity, and light—but with shade rather than direct sunlight. Use a balanced feed periodically. With proper conditions the bloom can last eight to 10 weeks.

Classification

Paphiopedilum insigne (Lindley) Pfitzer 1888.

Paphiopedilum insigne

Paphiopedilum rothschildianum

This exquisite and rare terrestrial orchid from North Borneo grows at 3,600 feet (1,100 m) on steep slopes and cliff faces near or above running water, where it forms clumps. The leaves are suberect, narrowly elliptical, or ligulate, and 16 to 24 inches (40–60 cm) long.

The inflorescence is 26 to 30 inches (70–75 cm) tall and bears three or more flowers. The dorsal sepal is yellowish with white margins and marked with longitudinal dark purple or black stripes. The synsepalum is smaller with similar markings. The long narrow petals are yellowish green or pale green, striped longitudinally, and slightly tapered to the apex but not twisted. The slipper-shaped lip is purple or brown with ocher coloring at the top edge.

Cultivation

Grow in pots containing free-draining compost comprising 80 percent bark and 20 percent coarse peat substitute; additional charcoal, pumice, or perlag may be introduced. The compost must hold moisture but should not become wet. Stand pots on a pebble tray to maintain good humidity. Grow in warm, bright light, but not in direct sunlight, and ensure that there is good air movement. A balanced feed can be given periodically. Repot when the compost breaks down or every two years.

Classification

Paphiopedilum rothschildianum (Reichenbach f.) Pfitzer 1895.

Paphiopedilum rothschildianum

Other *Paphiopedilum* Species

Paphiopedilum godefroyae
from Thailand.

Paphiopedilum sukhakulii
from northeastern Thailand.

PAPHIOPEDILUM

Paphiopedilum malipoense from southern China to northern Vietnam.

Paphiopedilum concolor from China to Indochina.

398

Paphiopedilum Hybrids

Paphiopedilum lowii 'John Shinn'

Paphiopedilum 'Michael Koopowitz'

Phalaenopsis

DATA

Number of Species: About 60.

Classification: *Phalaenopsis* Blume C. L. 1825; tribe Vandeae, subtribe Sarcanthinae.

Form: Roots are fleshy and adventitious; in leafless species they bear chlorophyll. Leaves are broadest at apex, leathery, arranged in two rows, often twisted. The inflorescence is erect and can be long and arched, also short and erect; very showy, with few to many small to large flowers which can be long lasting. Petals and sepals are similar but the petals are wider; the lip is three-lobed, not hinged.

Distribution: Philippines, Malaysia, Southeast Asia, India, Formosa, Northern Australia, New Guinea.

Habitat: Mostly moist and humid locations in rain forests. Mainly epiphytic, some lithophytic.

The mothlike appearance of the flowers as they dance in a breeze gives this genus its name—*phalaina* is Greek for "moth," and *opsis* means "appearance." The flowers are very showy and range from white (with yellow or orange lip markings) through shades of pink. Some are fragrant. The inflorescence is long and arching, pendulous to short erect.

Thousands of hybrids have been developed commercially because the flowers are long lasting and large.

Cultivation

Phalaenopsis require intermediate to warm growing temperatures—minimum 59°F (15°C). They can be grown in pots with a medium to coarse bark chip compost; a little chopped sphagnum moss and charcoal lumps may be added but the medium must be free draining. They may also be grown on bark or wood blocks. Roots need a light wrap of moss when tying to bark or block. Another method is to grow them in baskets containing moss, topped up with coarse bark chips. All adventitious roots should be allowed to hang in the air. Plants need a good watering while growing and should be nearly dry before the next watering, but never allow the plants to dry out completely. Always drain excess water away before replacing them in their normal position. Never leave water in the crown of the plant or this will cause rot.

Feed with a general purpose liquid fertilizer, lowering the strength in winter. Every fourth watering, flush the compost through with clear water to remove salts that build up. Maintain humid conditions and good air movement around the plants. Good light is essential but avoid direct sunlight, which will burn the leaves.

Phalaenopsis bastianii is found in the Philippines.

Phalaenopsis equestris

A widespread epiphytic orchid from the Philippines, *Phalaenopsis equestris* survives from sea level up to 1,000 feet (300 m). Its leaves can be up to 8 inches (20 cm) in length and 2.5 inches (6.5 cm) wide. They are oblong elliptical to oblong ovate in shape, fleshy, and sometimes purple on the underside. This species produces a long arching inflorescence of some 10 to 15 flowers. Flowers are white to pale rose red; the lip is a deeper magenta red, moving to yellow or orange at its base.

Cultivation

Grow in a potting medium consisting mainly of conifer bark that contains some perlite, pumice, charcoal, and coarse peat substitute, which must be free draining. Plants grow better in baskets where the adventitious roots can be exposed to the air and humidity. It requires water all year—slightly less in winter—and should be kept moist and in good humidity. Liquid fertilizer may be given, but flush with plain water every four to six weeks to remove undissolved salts. This species prefers shade rather than direct sunlight, which will burn the leaves, especially when new growth is appearing. Too much shade will encourage long leaves and discourage flowering.

Classification

Phalaenopsis equestris Reichenbach f. (*Phalaenopsis rosea* Lindley *Stauroglottis equestris* Schaur)

Phalaenopsis equestris was originally found on the island of Luzon by Meyer and was finally described by Schaur in 1843. In 1849 it was transferred into *Phalaenopsis* by H. G. Reichenbach (Linnaeus p.847).

Phalaenopsis equestris

Phalaenopsis hieroglyphica

The epiphytic *Phalaenopsis hieroglyphica* occurs in the Philippines (Palawan and Polillo areas only). It has coarse fleshy roots, and its leaves are up to 12 inches (30 cm) long and 2.5 inches (6.5 cm) wide, with an acute or obtuse tip. The inflorescence is suberect to arching, with many flowers. The bracts are ovate to hooded in shape, 0.2 inch (5 mm) long. The flowers are white or ocher in color, with cinnamon hieroglyphic markings or spots. The whitish lip is flushed pink or purple, three-lobed, up to 1 inch (2.5 cm) long, and 0.75 inch (1.8 cm) wide, with a cushionlike central ridge. The cylindrical column is 0.5 inch (1.2 cm) long and slightly arched.

Cultivation

This orchid is best grown in baskets in a free-draining compost comprising bark with pumice, perlite, coarse peat substitute, or charcoal in smaller quantities. The adventitious roots should be allowed to hang freely in the air, and good air movement is required. Water *Phalaenopsis hieroglyphica* well during the growing season, reducing the amount of water in winter. Feed with a liquid fertilizer but flush with clean water every four to six weeks. Direct sunlight should be avoided so as not to burn the new leaf growth or the older leaves. Give good light but shade the plant from harsh sun. The minimum winter temperature should be 59°F (15°C).

Classification

Phalaenopsis hieroglyphica
Reichenbach f., Sweet.

The original description by H. G. Reichenbach in 1887 (Gardeners Chronicle ser. 3,2 p.586). H. Sweet raised *Phalaenopsis hieroglyphica* to specific rank (A. O. S. Bulletin, p.36) in 1969.

Phalaenopsis hieroglyphica

Phalaenopsis stuartiana

Found in the Philippines, *Phalaenopsis stuartiana* grows at elevations of up to 900 feet (300 m). It is epiphytic and blooms in early winter or spring. Its 36-inch- (91-cm-) long, arched, pendent inflorescence can carry as many as 100 fragrant flowers. The white coloration of the flowers and the strongly masked lip callus differentiate this orchid from *P. schilleriana*. The leaves are few in number and grow to 14 inches (35 cm) long and 3 inches (8 cm) wide. They are green with silvery or gray mottling.

Cultivation

Phalaenopsis stuartiana is best grown in pots, on rafts, or in baskets. In pots or baskets the main compost ingredient is bark with added perlite and charcoal. Grow in humid conditions. On rafts, use sphagnum moss around the roots to hold a little moisture but do not keep wet, although humid conditions should be maintained. Spray the roots on rafts daily, and soak once a week. A liquid feed may be given, flushed through with clean water every four to six weeks. Do not mist the plants when temperatures are below 65°F (18°C), since this can cause root rot from water retained in the root axils.

Propagation can be by plantlets or meristem culture. *Phalaenopsis stuartiana* can also be raised easily from seed. Pot or mount while the root tips are active and growing, taking care not to damage the roots.

Classification

Phalaenopsis stuartiana Reichenbach f. 1881

Working on behalf of Low and Low, W. Boxall collected this specimen from the island of Mindanao in 1881. Stuart Low sent it to Reichenbach, who named it *P. stuartiana* in that same year. It is treated by some authors as a variety of *P. schilleriana*.

Phalaenopsis stuartiana

Phalaenopsis violacea

The Violet Phalaenopsis, *Phalaenopsis violacea*, is found on the Malay Peninsula and the island of Sumatra. It is an epiphyte that requires warm conditions. Its leaves are fleshy, 8 to 10 inches (20–25 cm) long, 3 to 5 inches (7.5–13 cm) wide, and shiny dark green in color. The roots are stout and hairless, with a smooth surface. The inflorescence is jointed, stout, and usually 4 to 5 inches (10–13 cm) long. The rachis is zigzag shaped and flattened.

The flowers, which open successively, number two to seven along the length of the flowering stem. They are large—typically 2 to 3 inches (5–7.5 cm) in diameter. Flowers from peninsular Malaysia are an even pink color, while others are more greenish with some purple on the sepals and lip.

Because of its fragrant nature *P. violacea* is widely used for hybridizing.

Cultivation

Phalaenopsis violacea benefits from warm conditions with good humidity and deep shade. It is suitable for pots, rafts, or baskets, but must be planted in free-draining medium and kept moist, not wet. Never allow the plant to dry out. Water it well during the growing season, starting with a little at the first signs of growth, and gradually increasing the amount given. Feed with liquid fertilizer but flush with clean water every four to six weeks to remove excess salts.

Never cut off the inflorescence stem once the first flower has finished, because it will reflower along the stem successively, thus extending the flowering period. Repot when the root tips are growing, but avoid root damage when repotting or putting on a raft.

Classification

Phalaenopsis violacea Witte 1860.

Phalaenopsis violacea

Other *Phalaenopsis* Species

Phalaenopsis lowii from Myanmar
(Burma) to western Thailand.

Phalaenopsis amabilis
from Southeast Asia.

Phalaenopsis fasciata from the Philippines.

Phalaenopsis pulcherrima
from Southeast Asia.

Phalaenopsis bellina
from Borneo.

Phalaenopsis Hybrids

Phalaenopsis 'Mambo'

Phalaenopsis 'Sweetheart'

Phalaenopsis 'Happy Tater'

Phragmipedium

DATA

Number of Species: About 20.

Classification:
Phragmipedium Rolfe 1896;
tribe Phragmipedieae,
subtribe Phragmipediinae.

Form: Pseudobulbs lacking. Short
simple stems produce one or
more straplike unveined leaves
arranged in ranks either side of
the stem or in a fan. A terminal
unbranched inflorescence bears
two to six sequentially opening
blooms. Flowers have fused
lateral sepals forming a synsepal,
in front of which the lip is
shaped like a pouch or slipper,
with its edge curved inward. The
petals are often elongate and
the column is short with two
anthers bearing soft pollinia.

Distribution: From Mexico to
Brazil and Bolivia.

Habitat: Live as epiphytes,
lithophytes, or terrestrials in
moist forest and scrublands at
elevations ranging from 1,300
to 7,200 ft (400–2,200 m).

Lady's slipper orchids are closely related to *Cypripedium* and *Paphiopedilum*, but their large size and showy blooms distinguish them and make them popular with cultivators. There are a number of widely grown hybrids. All members of this genus are listed on Appendix I of the Convention on the International Trade in Endangered Species (CITES), which places the tightest possible restrictions on exports and imports of all living or dead specimens. Cultivated stocks mean there is no longer a need for any of the rare wild plants to be collected or interfered with, but often the sites of natural stocks require protection from unscrupulous collectors.

Cultivation

Phragmipedium orchids are naturally cluster forming, and should be allowed to do so under cultivation—splitting them too often weakens the root stock considerably. Most species will do well in free-draining compost with added moss for moisture retention. Plants should be kept in intermediate conditions and partial shade, and most require regular watering all year round. A dilute balanced fertilizer should be applied at least weekly.

Phragmipedium pearcei originates from Ecuador and Peru, where it grows on rocks along streams and rivers and among trees at the edges of wet forest.

Phragmipedium besseae

Besse's Phragmipedium (*Phragmipedium besseae/Phragmipedium dalessandroi*) manages to combine strident color with subtle beauty—the dorsal sepal and petals are an incredible vivid orange red, while the lip may be pale peach streaked with apricot to bright red streaked with yellow. The species was discovered on the eastern slopes of the Andes mountains of Peru in 1981 by Elizabeth Locke Besse, for whom it is named. It grows at about 3,300 to 5,000 feet (1,000–1,500 m), usually on mossy rock faces where it receives a steady trickle of water all year around.

The years following its discovery saw a disgraceful scramble by illegal collectors, and the original site was all but destroyed. The species might have been lost completely were it not for the preservation of some seeds. No other member of the genus has similar colors and, as a result, the species has been used extensively in hybrids.

Cultivation

Phragmipedium besseae is by far the thirstiest of its genus and likes to have its feet wet continuously throughout the year, requiring daily watering and a moisture-retentive mossy compost mix. It should be placed in dappled or semishade under intermediate, humid conditions and fed weekly with very dilute balanced fertilizer.

Classification

Phragmipedium besseae Dodson & Kuhn 1981.

Phragmipedium besseae

Phragmipedium caudatum

This is a relatively widespread species, found growing on tree branches or mossy rock faces at moderate altitudes throughout much of southern Central America and northern South America. The plants typically form clusters. Each plant produces just one 24-inch- (60-cm-) long straplike leaf and an erect inflorescence with up to six remarkable flowers. The lip is delicate greenish yellow, tended above and below by an elongated dorsal sepal and synsepal, both of which have pale green veins and are often twisted. The extraordinary petals are superelongate, forming a pair of twisting red brown "tails" up to 20 inches (50 cm) long.

Cultivation

This rather large species should be allowed to form large clusters and be given plenty of headroom for its flowering stems. It can be potted in a pot or basket but drainage must be excellent, since it will not tolerate water-logging. The flowers appear in the fall, after which the plant requires a rest from watering. Intermediate temperatures and partial shade suit the species well.

Classification

Phragmipedium caudatum (Lindley) Rolfe 1896.

Phragmipedium caudatum

Physosiphon

DATA

Number of Species: About 7.

Classification: *Physosiphon*
Lindley 1835; tribe Epidendreae,
subtribe Pleurothallidinae.

Form: Somewhat variable. Most are
small plants in which clustered
pseudobulbs are partly sheathed
by single elongate leaves. Most
produce many very small flowers
on long racemose inflorescences
that rise from the leaf axil. The
flowers resemble those of certain
Pleurothallis species, but are
distinguished in having a tube
formed by fusion of the three
sepals. As with *Pleurothallis*,
there are always two pollinia.

Distribution: Tropical regions of
the Americas; Mexico to Brazil.

Habitat: Epiphytic in a wide
variety of forested habitats from
sea level to mountains of about
9,000-ft (2,700-m) elevation.

Since its first description by the legendary John Lindley, this genus of miniature neotropical epiphytes has frequently been treated as a synonym of the huge and poorly defined mixed-bag genus *Pleurothallis*. Taxonomic reshuffling of the latter in the light of molecular evidence, however, may well see *Physosiphon* reinstated. For horticultural purposes it has been helpful to retain the name regardless.

Cultivation

The variability of habitats favored by species in this group means there are few hard and fast rules for growing them all. They range from warm- to cool-tolerant species and they flower sporadically at different times of the year. As epiphytes, however, most will require restricted root space and excellent drainage, so small pots or mossy slab media are recommended. The plants require regular watering, dilute feed throughout the year, and annual repotting.

Known as the Tube-forming Physosiphon, *Physosiphon tubatus (Stelis tubata)* is found growing epiphytically on oak trees in wet or dry forests in Central America.

Pleione

DATA

Number of Species: About 20.

Classification: *Pleione* David Don 1825; tribe Coelogyneae, subtribe Coelogyninae.

Form: Compact miniatures with egg-, bottle-, or spinning-top-shaped pseudobulbs bearing one or two unremarkable leaves that wither and drop seasonally. The appeal of the plant is in its disproportionately large showy flowers—generally just one but occasionally two blooms per plant. They are usually white, pink, or purple, sometimes yellow.

Distribution: South and East Asia from Nepal to Taiwan.

Habitat: Cool uplands and mountain ranges, often close to the snow line and as high as 14,000 ft (4,200 m) in some cases. Usually epiphytic, on trunks or branches of moss-covered trees; also lithophytic on rock faces.

Originally classified within the closely related genus *Coelogyne*, these Himalayan specialists appear to put all their energies into their spectacular blooms. At other times the plants are wholly unremarkable. Usually a single show-stopping flower appears along with, or sometimes before, new growth from the psuedobulbs. The genus is widely cultivated and hybridized—more than 30 hybrids have been registered to date. The generic name honors Pleione, the mother of the Pleiades, according to Greek mythology. They are sometimes known as Himalayan crocuses or peacock orchids because of the large and often ornately decorated lip.

Cultivation

Pleione orchids do well in temperate climates and most benefit from being kept outside under glass in winter. They should be grown in shallow containers with a loose, light, medium comprising chopped sphagnum moss, fibrous compost, or loam mixed with perlite or granular polystyrene and crushed charcoal. The result is a moisture-retentive mix that does not become waterlogged or compacted around the roots. The plants should be repotted in fresh medium each year. Regular watering and feeding with a dilute nitrogen-rich fertilizer should be maintained throughout the growing season, and suspended from late fall to early winter.

Occurring in South and Southeast Asia, *Pleione praecox* lives in moss or on moss-covered branches at altitudes of 4,000 to 11,300 feet (1,200–3,400 m).

Pleione formosana

Named for its strong association with the island of Taiwan (formerly Formosa), but also occurring less commonly on mainland China, *Pleione formosana* is a compact alpine epiphyte of moderate altitudes, found growing naturally on mossy rocks and trees between 1,700 and 8,300 feet (500–2,500 m). A single large leaf measuring 12 inches (30 cm) long arises from a flask-shaped pseudobulb. The lone flower is usually pink—sometimes white—and up to about 2.8 inches (7 cm) across. It is held about 2.5 inches (6 cm) above the pseudobulb.

Cultivation

Pleione formosana should be repotted at the start of the growing season, ideally just before signs of new growth appear. A shallow pan and mixed lightweight compost that is water retentive are ideal. The plants need bright light during the growing season and can be kept outdoors or close to a well-lit window all summer.

Regular watering is essential, and feeding with a dilute nitrogen-rich fertilizer should begin as soon as new growth is observed. Switch to potassium-rich feed toward the end of the season. Both feeding and watering should be reduced as the leaves wither in the fall, and the pan should be allowed to become almost dry over winter. At this stage the dry pseudobulbs can be removed from the pot for storage.

Classification

Pleione formosana Hayata 1911.

Pleione formosana

Pleione maculata

The Spotted Pleione, *Pleione maculata*, is another popular cool- to cold-growing species, but unlike *P. formosana* it blooms in the fall. The species is native to undisturbed cloud forests of Vietnam and Thailand, at altitudes exceeding 6,600 feet (2,000 m). It is greatly admired for its blooms, the petals and sepals of which are bright white, but the inside of the lip is strikingly patterned with harlequin yellow and pinkish or purplish red. The effect is that of the most delicate hand-painted porcelain. The popular *Pleione x lagenaria* is a hybrid of this species and *P. praecox.*

Cultivation

An ideal species for the novice grower, the Spotted Pleione is easy to grow but highly rewarding. It fares well on a bright but unheated windowsill in temperate climates and will produce its exquisite blooms just as many other houseplants are past their best. It can be grown in a shallow container or even a basket, rooted in a medium of equal parts standard orchid mix, chopped sphagnum moss, and perlite. It should be watered and fed regularly with dilute balanced fertilizer until the leaves wither, then repotted at the end of the growing season in later winter.

Classification

Pleione maculata (Lindley) Lindley & Paxton 1851–52.

Pleione maculata

Pleione Hybrids

Pleione formosana
'Snow White'

Pleione 'Zeus Weistein'

Pleurothallis

DATA

Number of Species: About 1,000.

Classification: *Pleurothallis* Robert Brown 1813; tribe Epidendreae, subtribe Pleurothallidinae.

Form: Hugely variable, from miniature mossy epiphytes to giant terrestrials, pleurothallids adopt almost all growth habits and range from trailers and scramblers to erect clustered or solitary plants. Single leaves, variable in shape and size, arise from rhizomes; pseudobulbs are absent. The flowers are highly variable in size, color, and shape, and may bloom singly or on many-flowered stems. There are always two pollinia.

Distribution: Tropical regions of the Americas, from the southern United States to Brazil, in particular the Andes mountains of Colombia and Ecuador.

Habitat: From sea level to mountains 10,000 ft (3,000 m) or more above sea level; in warm to cool conditions. Most species are epiphytic or lithophytic.

This huge and unwieldy group, known loosely as bonnet orchids, has recently undergone a major taxonomic revision. Prior to this the genus was something of a catchall for members of the Plerothallidinae that could not be clearly assigned to other existing genera. At one time an estimated 1,800 species had been described, although up to half of these were probably synonyms. Recent molecular studies suggest that several hundred species should be hived off into new genera, leaving a mere 600 or so species within *Pleurothallis*.

Cultivation

While many *Pleurothallis* orchids are easy to grow and make popular subjects for cultivation, the group's diversity means there are few hard and fast rules for their care and maintenance. The majority of species will grow in pots in free-draining compost and most, but not all, need year-round watering and feeding.

This miniature epiphyte is *Pleurothallis luteola (Acianthera luteola)*, known as the Yellow Pleurothallis. It originates from Brazil, and its flowers measure just 0.15 to 0.2 inches (4–5 mm) across.

Pleurothallis alveolata

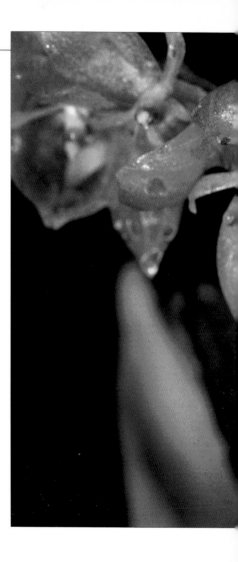

This diminutive epiphyte from upland regions of Ecuador is notable for its tiny flowers—each bloom is approximately 0.1 inch (2.5 mm) in diameter, with membranous sepals and petals. The epithet *alveolata* means "small cavity," and describes the tiny bowl formed by the fused lateral sepals. They encircle the dark pink or red lip, which is sometimes unflatteringly likened to the bloody socket left by an extracted tooth. The flowers bloom by the dozen or more and are arranged either side of a long raceme.

Cultivation

Despite being a mountain species, the equatorial range of *Pleurothallis alveolata* means it requires intermediate to warm growing conditions. It can be potted in light epiphyte compost or mounted on a tree fern or bark slab. It should be watered daily and fed weekly with a dilute, balanced fertilizer. The plant should be exposed to low to moderate indirect light and good air flow. The compost should not be allowed to become stale, and careful annual repotting is recommended.

Classification

Pleurothallis alveolata Luer 1976.

Pleurothallis alveolata

Pleurothallis (Acronia) dilemma

This is a strange little plant with a short and lively horticultural history. In the few short years since it was first scientifically described in 2001 it has become a hot favorite among amateur and professional growers, thanks to its extraordinary succulent "twinned string-bean" leaves and small, blood-blister flowers, which measure just 0.6 inch (1.5 cm) across. It also is one of the species that has recently been reassigned to a new genus, namely *Acronia* (as *A. dilemma*), following molecular studies in 2005.

The epithet *dilemma* invokes the word's original meaning—"two-horned"—which came to signify a problem caused by having to make one of two choices. In the plant it refers to the basal horns of the long tapering leaves. The flowers open directly between the horns. The plant grows naturally on mossy tree trunks and branches in cool uplands of Ecuador, between 6,000 and 6,600 feet (1,800–2,000 m).

Cultivation

This extraordinary plant requires cool moderately lit conditions that mimic its natural habitat. It should be grown on a bark or tree-fern mount, watered daily while growing, and fed weekly with dilute balanced fertilizer.

Classification

Pleurothallis dilemma Luer 2001
(*Acronia dilemma* [Luer] Luer 2005).

Pleurothallis (Acronia) dilemma

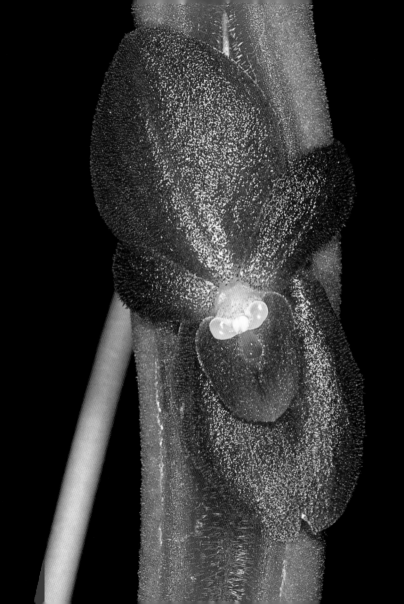

Polystachya

DATA

Number of Species: About 150.

Classification: *Polystachya*
William Hooker 1824;
tribe Polystachyeae.

Form: Small compact orchids with small pseudobulbs that vary in shape from species to species. They sprout in clusters from a creeping basal rhizome. The leaves are mostly long and tapering; the flowers are small and highly variable in color. They bloom on tall inflorescences, inverted so that the lip faces upward. The lateral sepals fuse to form a mentum, or "chin."

Distribution: Mostly species are African, but a few occur on Madagascar and in Asia and the Americas.

Habitat: Most are epiphytes, found growing on trees in tropical forests. Different species occur at different altitudes, from sea level to high mountains.

This large and diverse group, dominated by African endemics, was first described more than 180 years ago, but new species are still being discovered to this day. *Polystachya* is by far the largest genus of epiphytic orchids in Africa, and they are recognized by their candlelike terminal inflorescences of small "upside-down" flowers. The name derives from the Greek *poly* meaning "many" and *stachya* ("spikes"), referring to the numerous flower spikes.

Cultivation

Polystachya species are popular with amateur growers. They do best in small- to medium-sized pots, bedded in an epiphyte compost mix containing bark for texture, sphagnum moss for water retention, and charcoal or granular polystyrene to keep the mix light and open. High-altitude species are tolerant of cooler conditions than those from lower levels, but the group's naturally wide ecological range means there is effectively a *Polystachya* for all conditions.

Polystachya bella 'Kyong Hee'; in the wild this species occurs only in Kenya and favors damp, shady rainforest habitats.

Polystachya pubescens

A strikingly attractive species from eastern South Africa and Swaziland, *Polystachya pubescens* is prized by growers for its tiny yellow flowers, each of which is less than 1 inch (about 2 cm) in diameter but with intense yellow petals and sepals that bloom in clusters of up to a dozen. The lateral sepals are accented with fine red lines and the lip has several long white hairs on its upper surface. The plant is epiphytic or lithophytic in cool low-lying forest with high rainfall or swampy ground.

Cultivation

Polystachia pubescens can be mounted on slab media such as tree fern or bark block, but usually does better potted in a light, fir-bark compost and charcoal mix, with a layer of sphagnum to hold moisture close to the roots. It should be grown indoors, or outside in cool to intermediate conditions, placed in a lightly shaded airy spot, and watered and fed with dilute fertilizer regularly throughout the growing season. During winter watering should be suspended until the plant shows signs of new growth.

Classification

Polystachya pubescens (Lindley)
Reichenbach f. 1863.

Polystachya pubescens

Polystachya vulcanica

In the tropical African countries of Rwanda, Uganda, and the Democratic Republic of the Congo, this delightfully demure orchid grows in humid upland forests at elevations of between 5,400 and 10,000 feet (1,650–3,000 m), where it clings to mossy trees and rock outcrops. It is a typically compact plant with tapering green leaves sheathing clustered pseudobulbs that give rise to dainty 1- to 3-inch (2.5–7.5-cm) flower spikes bearing up to five delicate inverted flowers. The lip is purple or yellow, the column is purple, and the sepals and petals are white. The species now includes *P. aconitiflora*, which was once treated as a separate species.

Cultivation

The plant needs cool to moderate conditions, indirect or dappled sunlight, and good air movement. It should be watered daily and benefits from regular misting. Dilute fertilizer should be delivered as long as the plant shows signs of flowering or active growth. The flowers bloom sporadically throughout the year.

Classification

Polystachya vulcanica Kraenzle 1923.

Polystachya vulcanica

444

Promenaea

Number of Species: About 14.

Classification: *Promenaea* Lindley 1843; tribe Cymbidieae, subtribe Stanhopeinae.

Form: Compact plants with prominent pseudobulbs. The pseudobulbs are sheathed by the leaves, which give rise to single flowered inflorescences from their axils. The flowers are large relative to the size of the plant and vary in color from species to species. The tepals are broadly similar in size and shape, the lip has three lobes, a large central lobe, and two smaller laterals that stand erect like sentries either side of the stout column. There are four pollinia.

Distribution: Central and southern Brazil.

Habitat: Members of this genus usually grow as epiphytes or lithophytes in moderate humid forests from sea level to 5,600 ft (1,700 m).

This small group is named for Promeneia, the eldest of three priestesses who tended the oracle, or shrine, of Dodona in ancient Greece—the priestesses went barefoot and slept on bare ground. Like their namesake, these attractive orchids sometimes grow on bare rock, rooted in small cracks and crevices; more usually, they grow on trees. The flowers are decorative and large relative to the size of the plant.

Cultivation

Only two species are cultivated widely, *Promenaea xanthina* and *P. stapelioides*. Both are popular for their small size, and can be grown in standard epiphyte compost mixes in small freely draining pots with some chopped sphagnum moss to prevent the roots ever becoming completely dry. The plants should be watered daily and placed somewhere where they will be exposed to moderate to bright light, intermediate temperatures and good air flow.

Promenaea xanthina is a native of southern Brazil, where it grows at an altitude of about 5,600 feet (1,700 m). This tiny rock- or tree-dwelling plant has just one or two yellow flowers measuring about 1.7 inches (4 cm) across.

Prosthechea

Number of Species: About 100.

Classification: *Prosthechea* Knowles and Westcott 1838; tribe Epidendreae, subtribe Laeliinae.

Form: Generally delicate-looking orchids with one to five rather flimsy leaves sprouting from spindle-shaped pseudobulbs. The flowers are variable, most are medium sized and usually bloom "upside down," the lip uppermost. The sepals and petals are generally similar but size, shape, and color vary greatly from species to species.

Distribution: Central and northern South America from Mexico to Brazil; also in Florida.

Habitat: Most grow on trees in tropical forests from sea level to about 8,700 ft (2,600 m).

Although the genus *Prosthechea* was first described in the 1830s, most of the species listed in it today have been classified previously as members of the similar genera *Encyclia* and *Epidendrum*. The revision brings together species with inverted flowers, leaving those with conventionally oriented blooms in their original groupings. As is often the case, the old classification is still used by many people in commercial horticulture.

Cultivation

Prosthechea orchids grow well in pots or baskets using standard epiphyte composts with a little chopped sphagnum moss to improve moisture retention. They require bright but indirect sunlight, moderate to high humidity, and good air movement. During the growing season they should be watered daily and fed at least once a week with dilute balanced fertilizer. Feeding and watering should both be reduced in winter when the plants are not blooming or actively growing.

Prosthechea fragrans has long-lasting, spring-flowering blooms which, as its name suggests, give off a fragrant perfume. It is found throughout South America and north to Mexico in Central America.

Prosthechea cochleata

Commonly known as the Clamshell, or Cockleshell, Orchid, *Prosthechea cochleata* has two synonyms: *Encyclia cochleata* and *Epidendrum cochleatum*. This popular and distinctive species has a wide natural distribution in swampy forests from Florida through Mexico to Venezuela and Colombia. It is also found on several islands of the West Indies. It occurs at a wide range of altitudes, from sea level to around 6,700 feet (2,000 m).

Each pseudobulb gives rise to two or three straplike leaves and a branching inflorescence up to 20 inches (50 cm) long. The flowers are large but delicate, with a broad lip that can be purple or yellow with purple spots and veins. The inferior tepals are pale and slender.

The Florida subspecies is unique in having three anthers bearing large quantities of pollen. Elsewhere, the species has just one anther. Botanists speculate that the Florida stock may be the descendants of a single plant, which could have arrived as a windblown seed or been carried by a bird from the West Indies.

Cultivation

The broad habitat requirements of this robust orchid and its succession of delightful flowers that bloom throughout the year make it an easy and popular species to cultivate. It can be potted in almost any bark-based epiphyte mix and grown indoors or outside under some shade. Moderate to bright indirect light is ideal, but the species may adapt to lower light conditions and still bloom. Watering and feeding can continue as long as the plant is showing signs of active growth, but should be eased off during periods of dormancy.

Classification

Prosthechea cochleata (Linnaeus) W. E. Higgins 1997.

Prosthechea cochleata

Prosthechea vitellina

The spectacular *Prosthechea vitellina* (*Encyclia vitellina*) is a high-altitude specialist growing naturally in a wide range of montane forest and scrub in Mexico and Guatemala at moderate to high altitudes of 5,000 to 8,700 feet (1,500–2,600 m). The beautiful long-lasting flowers bloom between four and 12 at a time on inflorescences about 12 inches (30 cm) long. The petals and sepals are vivid orange to red and the lip is bright yellow with an orange or red tip.

Cultivation

Prosthechea vitellina requires cooler conditions than other members of the group, reflecting its montane habitat. It can flower at any time of the year, and watering and feeding should be tailored to the needs of the individual plant—this should be done regularly during the flowering and growth period and reduced during periods of apparent dormancy, usually in winter. This orchid can be grown in a small pot or on a slab and kept indoors or outside in temperate climates. It should be protected from direct sunlight.

Classification

Prosthechea vitellina (Lindley)
W. E. Higgins 1997.

Prosthechea vitellina

Psychopsis

DATA

Number of Species: About 4.

Classification: *Psychopsis* Rafinesque 1838; tribe Cymbidieae, subtribe Oncidiinae.

Form: Pseudobulbs give rise to a single internode and a single reddish brown leaf marked with green spots and blotches. The flower spikes arise from the axils of elongate sheaths subtending the internode. Several single flowers bloom in succession at the tip of each spike. The dorsal sepal and petals are very narrow, while the lateral sepals are large and showy with ruffled or crisped margins. The lip is greatly expanded, with similarly crisped edges. All petals and sepals are boldly patterned in red and gold.

Distribution: Central and northern South America from Costa Rica to Peru.

Habitat: Low-lying forests between sea level and 2,600 ft (800 m) in humid to wet conditions that allow them to root without soil in branches of trees and shrubs.

It is not hard to see why these striking plants are known as butterfly orchids—even the generic name translates directly from Greek as "butterfly-like." They were formerly classified within the vast genus *Oncidium* and are still listed as such by some authorities.

Cultivation

Butterfly orchids do well under cultivation but require regular maintenance and can be unforgiving of neglect. If the potting medium is allowed to become stale they will die very suddenly, so regular feeding with dilute fertilizer and annual repotting are recommended.

Psychopsis (Psychopsiella) limminghei is a dwarf epiphyte in which the flowers grow to a maximum of 1.5 inches (4 cm); it comes from Brazil and Venezuela.

Psychopsis krameriana

Anative of low-lying forests from Costa Rica to Ecuador, Kramer's Butterfly Orchid (*Psychopsis krameriana/Oncidium kramerianum*) is popular with cultivators but can be a challenge to maintain. Cultivated plants can be expected to produce between five and eight single blooms in succession from an inflorescence. The flowers have the narrow dorsal sepal and petals typical of the genus, and the lower lip has a large patch of bright yellow at the center.

Cultivation

This species can be grown in a small basket or on a slab. Fast drainage and broadly consistent year-round conditions are essential. The plants require regular watering (up to twice a day or more on slabs in warm weather) and feeding with dilute, balanced fertilizer, with slightly reduced watering in winter. The roots should not be allowed to remain waterlogged, nor should they ever dry out completely. When growing the orchid in a basket, a fast-draining but desiccation-resistant medium containing sphagnum moss or perlite and charcoal is ideal.

Low to moderate light conditions are preferable, but the plants will tolerate bright light provided humidity and air movement are high, mimicking conditions in the higher branches of cloud-forest trees. Do not cut the flower spikes because blooming is sequential.

Classification

Psychopsis krameriana (Reichenbach f.) H. G. Jones 1975.

Psychopsis krameriana

Pterostylis

DATA

Number of Species: About 150.

Classification: *Pterostylis* Robert Brown 1810; tribe Diurideae, subtribe Pterostylidinae.

Form: Members of this diverse group of deciduous orchids grow alone or in vegetatively reproducing colonies. The leaves sprout in rosettes from small tuberous roots. The flowers are characteristically hooded with long points or tails on the sepals, a touch-sensitive lower lip, and four distinct pollinia. Both petals and sepals have somber red or green coloration.

Distribution: Mainly temperate Australia, with a few species extending into New Zealand, New Guinea, and New Caledonia.

Habitat: Cool temperate forests.

Commonly known as greenhoods, these unusual orchids live up to their somewhat sinister appearance by trapping insects such as mosquitoes and gnats. The lip is hinged and swings backward when an insect lands on it. The only way the insect can escape is by pushing its way past the column on which the four sticky pollinia are mounted. The leaves and flower stems die back in summer, during which time the plants undergo a period of dormancy.

Cultivation

As a group, greenhoods are not widely cultivated outside Australia but they can be grown in free-draining pots. Regular repotting every two years will prevent overcrowding in colonial species. The tubers of dormant plants can be split and repotted.

Within Australia Pterostylis nutans *ranges from northern Queensland to South Australia and Tasmania, and as far south as New Zealand. Its 12-inch- (30-cm-) tall stem bears a single small flower on the end.*

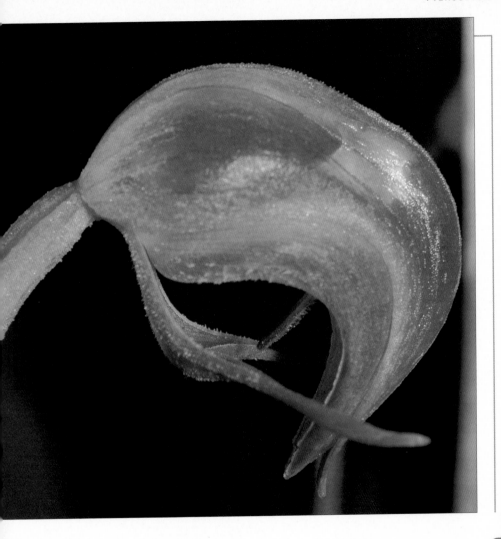

Pterostylis curta

A stout colonial species, *Pterostylis curta* is commonly known as the Blunt Greenhood. It is the type species for the whole genus—the first to be scientifically described. It has a widespread natural distribution down the east coast of Australia from Queensland to South Australia and Tasmania, where it is typically found in dry woodlands, sprouting up from gullies or small depressions where some moisture accumulates.

The 4-inch- (10-cm-) long oval leaves grow in rosettes of two to about six, from which the 12-inch- (30-cm-) tall flower spike emerges in late winter and bears a single hooded flower. The dorsal sepal has green and white stripes, tinged with brown toward the tip. The species is distinguished from its close relatives by its distinctive lip, the tip of which is always twisted to one side.

Cultivation

Pterostylis curta is the most widely cultivated member of the genus, especially outside Australia, where other *Pterostylis* species are rarely available. It is relatively easy to grow in intermediate conditions outside its native range and should be potted in a mixed loamy medium or a combination of sand and peat, to allow free drainage while resisting complete desiccation. The plants should be exposed to moderate to bright light and watered and fed regularly during the growing season but rested during the dormant phase.

Classification

Pterosylis curta Robert Brown 1810.

Renanthera

Number of Species: About 15.

Classification: *Renanthera* João de Loureiro 1790; tribe Vandeae, subtribe Sarcanthinae.

Form: *Renanthera* orchids have a scrambling vinelike growth habit, with roots and leaves sprouting at intervals along the vine and large, branching inflorescences bearing several dozen red, orange, or yellow flowers. The dorsal sepal and petals are of roughly uniform size and shape and usually curve slightly forward or backward. The lateral sepals are larger and less uniform, often with ruffled margins. The lip has three lobes; the middle lobe in particular may curve strongly backward.

Distribution: Southeast Asia and the Indo-Pacific from northeastern India to China, the Philippines, and New Guinea.

Habitat: Most members of the group grow in hot very humid lowland settings, including forests and gorges.

The genus was formally described and named by the Portuguese missionary João de Loureiro, a keen amateur naturalist. The name *Renanthera* is from the Latin meaning "kidney anther" and describes the shape of the four pollinia.

Cultivation

Renanthera orchids need warm conditions. In the tropics they will grow outdoors and will climb vigorously over trellises, pergolas, and trees. In temperate climates they will do well in humid greenhouses and solaria, where the larger species should be planted in free-draining baskets from which their vines can be allowed to cascade downward. Alternatively, they can be trained to climb a trellis or other structure. Smaller specimens can be planted in a pot with a small stake or trellis.

Endemic to the Philippines, *Renanthera philippinensis* is an epiphyte that requires full sun.

Renanthera citrina

This rare and recently discovered orchid is endemic to the North Vietnamese provinces of Cao Bang and Hoa Binh. It grows as an epiphyte in pine forest or as a lithophyte on limestone crags at moderate altitudes of about 2,600 to 4,000 feet (800–1,200 m). The scientific name *citrina* refers to the bright lemon yellow flowers. Both sepals and petals are narrow and marked with many dark purple spots. The flowers bloom simultaneously in inflorescences of 10 or so. The leaves are up to 5.5 inches (14 cm) long and leathery, and the flower stem is about 8 inches (20 cm) long.

The species is thought to be threatened by habitat loss and possible overcollecting. It is listed on Appendix II of the Convention on the International Trade in Endangered Species (CITES), which means it cannot be exported or imported without a license.

Cultivation

As a newly described species subject to export controls aimed at conserving wild specimens, *Renanthera citrina* is not yet readily available to amateur enthusiasts, although it has begun to feature in shows. It flowers from December to February. Like other small *Renanthera* species it should be grown in a freely draining pot and provided with a suitable structure over which to climb. It needs plenty of bright sunlight and moist growing conditions.

Classification

Renanthera citrina Averyanov 1997.

Renanthera citrina

Restrepia

Number of Species: About 50.

Classification: *Restrepia*
Humboldt, Bonpland, & Kunth
1815; tribe Epidendreae, subtribe
Pleurothallidinae.

Form: Small clump-forming plants
that lack pseudobulbs. The
distinctive flowers arise singly
from behind the waxy, light
green to reddish, ovate or oblong
leaves. The dorsal sepal is long
and very narrow with a clubbed
tip; the lateral sepals are fused
to form a single structure, the
synsepal, which is frequently cup
or trough shaped. The petals are
long and narrow, with clubbed
tips and delicate membranous
bases. The lip is small compared
to the synsepal and can be
tapering or violin shaped.

Distribution: Central and South
America from Mexico south as
far as northern Argentina, in the
Andes mountain range.

Habitat: Moist tropical forests.
Most species grow as epiphytes
or occasionally lithophytes.

The plants in this group are easily distinguished from other orchids
by their unusual flowers, but within the group the species can be
difficult to tell apart. It is likely that the current list of 50 or more
described species will be reduced to around 25 or 30 rather more
variable species. The name *Restrepia* is derived from that of José
Restrepo, a Colombian botanist.

Cultivation

These diminutive orchids are relatively easy to grow indoors or under
glass in cool to intermediate conditions and require relatively little
maintenance. They may be planted on slab media such as tree-fern
blocks, or in small pots in free-draining compost, mixed with sphagnum
moss to help maintain consistently moist conditions around the roots.
Partial sunlight is ideal—the leaves flush reddish under optimum light
conditions. Mature plants readily produce new plantlets or keikis, which
can be easily grown on. Alternatively, new plants can be successfully
propagated from leaf cuttings.

Restrepia guttulata produces single flowers in succession at the
base of the leaf. A South American species from Venezuela to Ecuador,
it is usually found at altitudes of 5,700 to 10,000 feet (1,700–3,000 m).

Restrepia brachypus

This dainty and charismatic orchid is relatively common in the Colombian and Ecuadorian Andes, between 5,000 and 10,500 feet (1,500–3,200 m), less so in Peru and Bolivia. The flowers are typical of the genus, with a long, slender, clavate (club-ended) dorsal sepal and petals, which are usually dark red. The fused lateral sepals form an elongate synsepal. They are gold with closely spaced longitudinal red stripes. The lip is pale red. A popular miniature with cultivators, *Restrepia brachypus* can flower at any time of year.

Cultivation

This dainty orchid can be grown on a block of cork or tree fern, or in a small pot with fir-bark compost and a layer of sphagnum. Good air flow around the plant is essential, but flowering seems to be enhanced by high humidity, and the plant should therefore be misted as the blooms begin to open. Dilute balanced fertilizer can be watered in but should also be delivered to any hairlike aerial roots by misting.

Classification

Restrepia brachypus Reichenbach f. 1886.

Restrepia brachypus

Restrepia condorensis

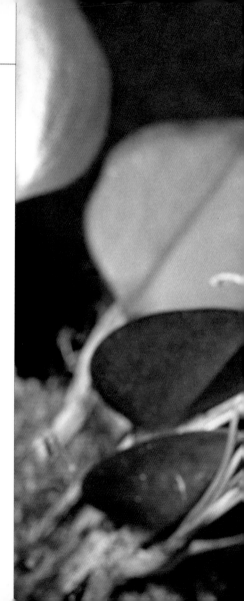

This rare and recently described species is native to the Cordillera del Condor, an unspoiled mountainous region in southeastern Ecuador, now part of a conservation area straddling the border with Peru to the south and protected jointly by both nations. The dainty flowers are no more than 0.8 inch (2 cm) across, and should be observed through a magnifying glass to be fully appreciated. The narrow, clavate dorsal sepal and petals all bear dark pink longitudinal stripes, and the synsepal is a vibrant pink with darker pink or red spots.

Cultivation

Restrepia condorensis is easy to grow in small pots or on slab media. It benefits from bright partial sunlight and will tolerate cool nighttime temperatures. The plant should be kept moist at all times and fed weekly with a dilute fertilizer. Plantlets sprouting from the leaf axils or leaf cuttings can be removed and planted in sphagnum moss, where they will take root in a few weeks or months.

Classification

Restrepia condorensis Luer & R. Escobar 1996.

Restrepia condorensis

Rossioglossum

DATA

Number of Species: About 6.

Classification: *Rossioglossum*
Garay & Kennedy 1976; tribe
Cymbidieae, subtribe Oncidiinae.

Form: Each squat, laterally
compressed pseudobulb gives
rise to two or three leaves and
an inflorescence of between four
and 11 blooms. The flowers are
waxy and long lasting, with
striking petals and sepals usually
boldly patterned with bands of
dark red and yellow. The lip is
bright or pale yellow with a
number of reddish brown spots
concentrated at the lower
margin. The column bears
a pair of pollinia.

Distribution: Central America,
from Mexico in the north to
Panama in the south.

Habitat: All members of this group
grow as epiphytes, rooted on the
branches of trees in damp cloud
forests at moderate to high
altitudes of about 2,000 to
5,000 ft (600–1,500 m).

This relatively recently described group comprises species that
were all previously classified within the genus *Odontoglossum*.
The German botanist Rudolf Schlecter recognized that these six species
represented a distinct group, but it was not until the 1970s that they
were formally separated and placed in the new genus *Rossioglossum*,
named for the English plant collector John Ross. As a group they are
not widely cultivated.

Cultivation

Ideal growing conditions for *Rossioglossum* species include a free-
draining medium, bright light, and intermediate temperature. Cool
nighttime conditions will be tolerated, but not frosts. Watering should
be suspended for a short period after flowering.

The warm- to cool-growing *Rossioglossum splendens* comes from
the forests of southwestern Mexico. It produces five chestnut brown flowers
edged with yellow, each measuring about 6 inches (15 cm) in diameter.

Rossioglossum grande

The popular orchid *Rossioglossum grande* (*Odontoglossum grande*) is the only member of *Rossiglossum* that is commonly cultivated. Its dramatic flowers are large—up to 5 inches (13 cm) in diameter—and long lasting. The petals are dark red with yellow tips, while the sepals are marked with red tiger stripes on a yellow background. All are moderately ruffled at the margins. The lip is so pale as to be almost white. It is found from Mexico south to Honduras. In Guatemala the species is know as *boca de tigre*, the Tiger Orchid.

Cultivation

In order to re-create a naturalistic growing environment for this striking orchid, the roots should be moderately restricted in a smallish clay pot and the leaves exposed to bright light and high humidity. A mixed medium of fir-bark compost and perlite will provide excellent drainage and prevent the roots from becoming waterlogged. The plant should be fed regularly with a dilute balanced fertilizer, and the soil leached periodically to remove the accumulated minerals. A rest from watering will be beneficial in winter as the flowers fade.

Classification

Rossioglossum grande (Lindley) Garay & Kennedy 1976.

Rossioglossum grande

Sarcochilus

DATA

Number of Species: About 15.

Classification: *Sarcochilus* Robert Brown 1810; tribe Vandeae, subtribe Sarcanthinae.

Form: Compact, sometimes cluster-forming plants with no pseudobulbs, just a few leaves and up to four short racemes per growth. There can be up to 15 colorful fragrant flowers per stem, ranging from 0.25 to 2 in (0.6–5 cm) at most in diameter.

Distribution: Australasia; all but one is endemic to Australia.

Habitat: Very diverse. Different *Sarcochilus* species grow as epiphytes on trees and shrubs or as lithophytes in rocky crevices, everywhere from the cool damp temperate zones to the humid tropics.

Following their first description in the early 19th century, a flurry of new "species" from all over Australia and Southeast Asia were named. From almost 200 of these described species, botanists now recognize just 15. One occurs on New Guinea and nearby islands; the rest are all restricted to Australia, and it is there that *Sarcochilus* orchids are most commonly cultivated.

Cultivation

As a group, *Sarcochilus* orchids are tolerant of a broad range of cool to intermediate temperatures, although individual species have more specific requirements. They tend not to be frost hardy. They all require bright to moderate light, good air flow, and high humidity. They should be grown on a slab or basket and the roots should be kept moist but not waterlogged. The leaves wilt rapidly under water stress. Misting will benefit the plants, especially in very warm or very cool conditions. They should be fed with dilute balanced fertilizer during the growing season.

Sarcochilus ceciliae is a cluster-forming orchid that can be found on rocks in the mountains on Australia's east coast. Like other members of the genus, it requires bright light and good air flow in order to thrive.

Serapias

DATA

Number of Species: About 10.

Classification: *Serapias* Linnaeus 1753; tribe Orchideae, subtribe Orchidinae.

Form: Potentially large erect plants growing from two or more underground tubers. The leaves are long and shiny. The flowers are distinguished by a tonguelike lower lip that emerges from a tube- or helmet-shaped structure, the galea, formed from two sepals fused to one petal.

Distribution: The Mediterranean and southern Europe.

Habitat: Calcareous to acidic grasslands, light woodland, and scrub, from sea level to moderate altitudes.

Orchids in the genus *Serapias* are relatively common in southern Europe and occasionally grow as far north as northern France or the British Isles, where they are regarded as a novelty. The tubelike shape of their flowers is a pollination strategy—the dark space inside the tube is sheltered and usually slightly warmer than the ambient temperature, making an attractive place for insects to rest and even spend the night. The insect accesses the tube by walking up the tongue. By the time it emerges after its visit, the insect will have ripe pollinia firmly attached to its head or body.

Cultivation

Serapias orchids are not often cultivated, presumably because their flowers, while interesting, are neither numerous, showy, nor heavily scented. However, they can be grown easily under glass or outside even in cool temperate regions, although they do need some protection from frosts.

Typical of the genus, *Serapias neglecta* grows from underground tubers. It produces two to eight lilac-colored flowers measuring 1 to 1.5 inches (2.5–4 cm).

Serapias vomeracea

Known as the Long-lipped Tongue Orchid, or the Plowshare Orchid, this species is widespread from Portugal to Greece. It grows in wet grasslands, light pinewoods, olive groves, and alpine meadows from sea level up to about 3,300 feet (1,000 m) in the southern foothills of the Alps, close to the northern limit of its range in Switzerland. It is regarded as a weed throughout much of its range. The leaves are green to red and strongly veined, while the petals and sepals are red brown to purple, and the tube is reddish.

Cultivation

Serapias vomeracea is easy to grow outside or under glass. If kept outside all year in cool temperate climates it should be in a raised bed to protect it from ground frosts. In a container it will do well in a basic *Ophrys*-type compost mix. It needs strong light and regular watering.

Classification

Serapias vomeracea (N. L. Burman) Briquet 1910.

Serapias vomeracea

Sophronitis

DATA

Number of Species: About 70.

Classification: *Sophronitis* Lindley 1828; tribe Epidendreae, subtribe Laeliinae.

Form: Mostly small plants with deep-red flowers. The pseudobulbs are small and cylindrical and develop in densely packed clusters well spaced out along the rhizome. Each pseudobulb develops a single, elongate, leathery, slightly grayish green leaf and a single flower stem, which may bear one or more blooms depending on the species.

Distribution: Central South America (Brazil, Bolivia, Paraguay, and northeastern Argentina).

Habitat: Most *Sophronitis* species grow in rocky crevices on exposed mountainsides. Others take root in the rough bark or forks of trees and shrubs in humid woodlands. They grow at moderate to high altitudes of about 1,300 to 5,000 ft (400–1,500 m).

The name *Sophronitis* comes from the Greek *sophron*, meaning "modest." These orchids live up to their name, typically being small, which makes them popular with hobby culturists. The flowers, however, can hold their own in any company, with their typically scarlet or orange pigmentation. Until recent DNA studies revealed their true affiliation, most of the Brazilian species were placed in the genus *Laelia* and are still often sold as such, commercial horticulture being slow to react to scientific reclassification.

Cultivation

Sophronitis species fall into two categories for cultivation purposes. The "original" epiphytic species do well on rafts or slab media and benefit from year-round watering. The lithophytes, on the other hand, prefer small pots and fibrous, free-draining media that simulate the restricted conditions of their natural habitats. They should be positioned in bright light with good air circulation. Their roots should never be permitted to become waterlogged and should be allowed to dry out completely in winter.

An inhabitant of Brazil to northeastern Argentina, *Sophronitis cernua* is a rock- or tree-dwelling orchid that flowers in the fall.

Sophronitis coccinea

A native of southern and southeastern Brazil, *Sophronitis coccinea* (*Cattleya coccinea*) grows at altitudes between 2,000 and 3,000 feet (600–900 m) in the cloud forests that shroud seaward-facing slopes of coastal mountain ranges. The high humidity creates moist growing conditions all year round, and the trees and shrubs are draped in mosses and other epiphytes, including these small tufty orchids with their vivid crimson flowers. The scientific epithet *coccinea* has the same etymology as cochineal—the intense and precious red pigment made from the small insect of the same name by the Aztec and Maya peoples of South America.

Cultivation

Since it is an epiphytic native of cloud forests, *S. coccinea* requires very regular watering and will benefit from daily misting to simulate the dense mists that envelop its natural habitat every evening. Strong light will enhance the color of the flowers. In temperate climates watering can be reduced in winter, but the roots must never be allowed to dry out. The plant should be repotted annually in a fibrous medium with a layer of sphagnum moss over the top to hold in moisture. Feeding with a balanced fertilizer should take place every two to three weeks in the growing season.

Classification

Sophronitis coccinea (Lindley) Reichenbach f. 1862.

Sophronitis coccinea

Sophronitis crispa

This is one of the many "new" species of *Sophronitis*, still often sold as *Laelia crispa*. It is typically a small epiphytic plant, found growing in the forks of trees and rock crevices. When it grows at the top of tall trees or on exposed crags with strong sunlight, free drainage, and good air circulation, however, it can become relatively large.

It originates from tropical rain forests at about 1,300 to 5,000 feet (400–1,500 m) in a specific area of southeastern Brazil, centered on Rio de Janeiro state. The flowers are scented and long lasting, with narrow ruffled white petals and an ornate purple lip and yellow throat. They bloom in spring and summer in clusters of up to 10.

Cultivation

Sophronitis crispa can be grown successfully on a block of cork or tree fern, or in a free-draining basket with very loosely packed fibrous bark medium. It requires bright light and daily watering to thrive and should be hung up to maintain good airflow around the whole plant. Dilute fertilizer should be applied throughout the growing and flowering season, but in winter feeding can be suspended.

Classification

Sophronitis crispa (Lindley) C. Berg & M. W. Chase 2000.

Sophronitis crispa

Stanhopea

DATA

Number of Species: About 60.

Classification: *Stanhopea* Frost ex Hooker 1829; tribe Cymbidieae, subtribe Stanhopeinae.

Form: The leaves are leathery with longitudinal creases, prominent veins, and a distinct stem, or petiole, that sprouts singly from tall oval pseudobulbs arranged in clusters. The flowers are large, waxy, and fragrant but short-lived. They appear on pendulous inflorescences of six to 20 blooms. The lower lip is an elaborate structure that can be divided into three sections: the upper epichile, middle mesochile, and basal hypochile.

Distribution: Central and South America from Mexico to Brazil.

Habitat: *Stanhopea* species typically occur as epiphytes in crevices on tree trunks in damp forests between 650 and 7,200 ft (200–2,200 m). They can also become established at ground level on steep slopes or embankments.

These unusual orchids are known for their spectacular large flowers, which normally hang below the plants. *Stanhopea* species regularly appear on emblems and special-edition stamps in their native countries. The leaves and growth habits of most members of the genus are very similar, and even experts can struggle to identify them to species when not in bloom. The genus was named for the Earl of Stanhope, a British patron of botany and president of the Medico-Botanical Society of London in the early 1800s.

Cultivation

In the wild *Stanhopea* trail from trees and steep slopes. The best way to approximate this natural habit is by planting them in a wire hanging basket with a layer of fibrous matting or compost or on a suspended slab of cork or tree fern. The plants do well in intermediate temperatures but need bright light, high humidity, and year-round watering.

A lover of moist conditions, *Stanhopea oculata* occurs on rocks, trees, or on the ground in the rain forests of Mexico, northern Brazil, and Colombia, at altitudes of about 2,300 to 5,000 feet (700–1,500 m).

Stanhopea tigrina

A large epiphytic species from Mexico, *Stanhopea tigrina* (*S. nigroviolacea*) is admired for its large fragrant tiger-striped flowers, which dominate in a great many cultivated hybrids. The flowers are produced just two at a time and open up to about 7 inches (18 cm) across. The petals are waxy, pale yellow to orange, with dramatic dark brown spots and speckles on the typically convoluted lip. The flowers open downward, toward the ground. The leaves are large, too—up to 14 inches (35 cm) long and 4 inches (10 cm) wide.

Cultivation

Like all *Stanhopea* species, this one can be grown in any compost recommended for epiphytic orchids, but it must be planted in a mesh basket, lined with bark or fibrous medium that allows the flower spike to penetrate and emerge beneath the plant. It favors cool to intermediate growing conditions and can be kept outside or indoors in partial shade. The roots should not be allowed to dry out, although watering should be reduced slightly in winter.

Classification

Stanhopea tigrina Bateman ex Lindley 1838.

Stanhopea tigrina var. *negroviolacea* 'Eddon II'

Stanhopea wardii

This potentially large species grows from trees or rock crevices in the humid cloud forests of Central America and northern South America. The leaves—up to 5.5 inches (14 cm) wide and twice as long—sprout singly from tall, compressed oval pseudobulbs. Up to 10 large heavily scented flowers bloom in a pendulous cluster below the plant. The petals and sepals are pale yellow with brown freckles. The lip structure is complex, resembling an insect—the pale mesochile and epichile mimic body and legs, and there are distinct red eyespots on the yellow hypochile.

Cultivation

The plant should be grown in an open mesh basket lined with fibrous medium and packed with epiphytic orchid compost. It can be kept outside in spring and summer but needs to be indoors during a temperate winter. Regular watering throughout summer is essential to keep the medium moist, but it can be allowed to dry out a little in winter. A dilute fertilizer can be applied during the growing season.

Classification

Stanhopea wardii Loddiges ex Lindley 1838.

Stanhopea wardii

Stenoglottis

Number of Species: About 3 to 6.

Classification: *Stenoglottis*
Lindley 1836; tribe Orchideae,
subtribe Orchidinae.

Form: Tuberous roots give rise to a
rosette of deciduous leaves that
vary in length and color among
species; they usually bear reddish
brown to purple spots, which
also appear on the bracts. A
single flower spike arises from
each rosette and has many small,
white, pink, or purple flowers. The
inflorescence continues to grow
throughout the flowering season,
with new blooms opening at the
top, so that flowering lasts for
several months.

Distribution: Central, southern,
and eastern Africa.

Habitat: *Stenoglottis* species
usually grow on the ground or on
mossy logs in humid forests from
sea level to about 5,900 ft
(1,800 m). Occasionally
specimens take root in crevices
and forks of living trees.

Members of this small group of African orchids produce an elegant
display in spring and summer, after which they wither back,
becoming leafless and dormant over the winter. *Stenoglottis* translates
literally from Greek as "narrow tongue," and the name aptly describes
the elongated lip, which in most species is deeply lobed.

Cultivation

These elegant plants are relatively easy to grow in cool to intermediate
temperate conditions. They should be potted in small shallow containers,
using a mixture of leaf mold and coarse sand. They should be placed in
partial shade, kept moist, and fed regularly with dilute fertilizer during
the growing season, and rested after the leaves die in the fall.

Stenoglottis woodii is unusual in the genus for having white or
pale pink flowers. There can be up to 40 blooms on each plant. The
species has a limited distribution in Zimbabwe and South Africa.

Stenoglottis fimbriata

The type specimen for its genus, *Stenoglottis fimbriata* (*S. zambesiaca*), the Fringed Orchid, is the most widely occurring member of the group, with a natural distribution extending from the South African province of KwaZulu Natal to Tanzania in East Africa.

The size and appearance of the leaves are variable, with some specimens heavily spotted on the rosette leaves and bracts, while others are almost plain. The flower spike reaches up to 16 inches (40 cm) tall and bears 50 or more spotty pink or lilac flowers, with a distinctive three-lobed lip. They open sequentially in summer and fall. In some parts of Africa a preparation of the roots is used as an enema to cure flatulence.

Cultivation

In cooler climates the Fringed Orchid will do well indoors or in a greenhouse if protected from direct sunlight. It should be repotted every two years at the start of the dormant season (winter). The container should be shallow, with a gritty organic medium. The tuberous root cluster can be split when repotting. When the leaves die back in the fall, watering and feeding should be suspended until signs of new growth appear in the spring, with just an occasional drenching to avoid complete desiccation of the roots.

Classification

Stenoglottis fimbriata Lindley 1836.

Stenoglottis fimbriata

Thunia

DATA

Number of Species: About 6.

Classification: *Thunia*
Reichenbach f. 1852; tribe
Arethuseae, subtribe Thuniinae.

Form: *Thunia* orchids produce erect
canelike stems that grow up to
4 ft (1.2 m) tall. The stems bear
two ranks of elongate leaves. The
large flowers bloom from the top
of the cane in short drooping
clusters of up to 10, each
reaching 5 or 6 in (13–15 cm)
in diameter. The petals do not
open fully.

Distribution: South and East Asia
from India to southern China
and the Malay Archipelago.

Habitat: *Thunia* orchids are
ground dwellers, occurring
naturally in hill country. They
favor woodlands and cane fields.

S ometimes called bamboo orchids because of their canelike stems,
Thunia orchids were previously included within the genus *Phaius*
on account of their similar flowers. After three flowering seasons the
canelike stems die back but will regenerate the following year.

Cultivation

These unusual orchids are fairly easy to cultivate and will grow outside
in temperate climates if protected from extremes of temperature. Plants
should be potted in terrestrial orchid compost, placed in a moderately
shady spot, and watered sparingly but regularly throughout the growing
season. *Thunia* species are deciduous—the leaves drop in winter, after
which the pot should be allowed to dry out until new leaves begin to
sprout. This rest period is important. New stems can be cultivated from
old canes laid on sphagnum moss but will take three years to reach
maturity and produce flowers.

Thunia alba is a native of South and Southeast Asia. It grows on
rocks, on the ground, and in tree forks at altitudes of 3,300 to 7,700 feet
(1,000–2,300 m). It produces up to 10 large flowers during the summer.

Vanda

DATA

Number of Species: About 50.

Classification: *Vanda* Jones ex R. Br 1820; tribe Vandeae, subtribe Sarcanthinae.

Form: *Vanda* orchids vary greatly in size from dainty miniatures to erect plants reaching head height. Some grow rooted in the branches of trees or in rock crevices. The stems are sturdy, with a rather unruly looking abundance of leathery, straplike leaves. The flowers vary in color from vibrant yellow, pink, and red to cool blues and whites. They are moderately long lasting and sweetly scented.

Distribution: South and East Asia from the Indian subcontinent to China, Australia, and the Philippines.

Habitat: Mostly forests from sea level to more than 6,700 ft (2,000 m) in the foothills of mountain ranges. Many species are climbers and will grow clinging to trees or rocky surfaces, in full or dappled sun.

Orchids in the genus *Vanda* are so diverse that in the past some species were classified in separate genera. The attractive fragrant flowers make *Vanda* species popular with florists, and there are a great many hybrids, developed in efforts to minimize the rather rambling natural growth habit and produce a greater density of valuable blooms on a more compact plant.

Cultivation

Small plants can be grown in a basket or a pot, but larger *Vanda* species produce large stout roots that are not easily contained. Thus the plants are often grown in baskets with little to no compost with the roots simply hanging free. In such cases the plants need very regular watering and feeding. All *Vanda* orchids need strong sunlight and consistent growing conditions. Few of them cope well with daily or seasonal variations in temperature or humidity.

Vanda tricolor is a sweet-smelling epiphyte native to eastern Java and Bali, where it grows in branches of trees at altitudes of 2,300 to 5,500 feet (700–1,700 m). It is relatively easy to cultivate in the garden.

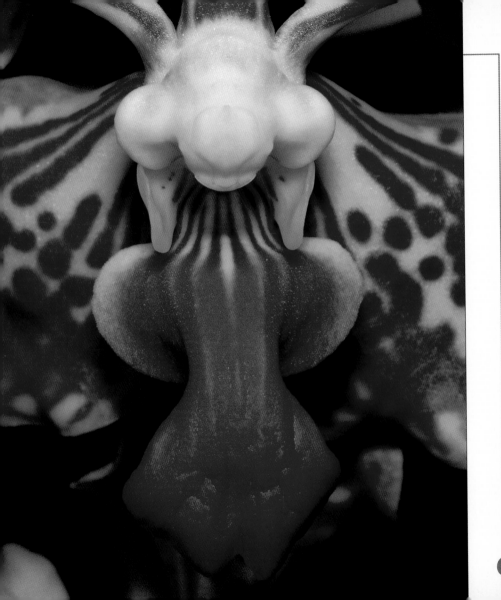

Vanda coerulea

A native plant of Himalayan forests, *Vanda coerulea*, the Blue Orchid, is one of few *Vanda* species from seasonal climates and one of very few truly blue orchids. It was discovered by the British botanist William Griffith in the 19th century, and its branching inflorescences and unusual color made it an instant must-have for plant collectors. Within decades it was becoming rare in the wild. The species is now listed on the Convention on the International Trade in Endangered Species (CITES), and key areas of habitat are protected. Enthusiasts can still enjoy the plant by cultivating it from seed.

Cultivation

Because of its high-altitude origins, the Blue Orchid is unusually tolerant of cool winter conditions. It needs plenty of moisture around the roots. This can be achieved by planting in a clay pot or basket with a layer of sphagnum moss over the roots and watering lightly every two to three days. Alternatively, daily misting will simulate the high humidity of the plant's native home and reduce the need for watering to once a week. Cultivated specimens can bloom at any time of year.

Classification

Vanda coerulea Griffith ex Lindley 1847.

Vanda coerulea

Vanda Hybrids

Vanda Gordon Dillon 'Blue Sapphire'

Vanda tricolor var. *suavis*

Vanda Pranerm Ornete x *Ascocenda* 'Butterfly'

Vanilla

DATA

Number of Species: About 60.

Classification: *Vanilla* Miller
1754; tribe Vanilleae, subtribe
Vanillinae.

Form: The scrambling vinelike
growth of *Vanilla* plants can
reach 100 ft (30 m) or more in
length. The roots that attach the
plant to structures such as trees
and rock faces arise in the axils
of fleshy, evenly spaced leaves,
as do the short flower stalks.
The flowers are large, pale,
and short lived and bloom
in quick succession.

Distribution: Tropical regions of
the Americas and Caribbean,
Africa, and Asia.

Habitat: Forest glades and
meadow edges exposed to the
sun, where suitable support
structures exist.

These orchids are better known for the culinary value of their pods than their blooms. The name is from the Spanish *vainilla*, meaning "little pod." Vanilla orchids occur naturally in Africa, Asia, and the Americas. The species most commonly used to produce vanilla pods for the kitchen is *Vanilla planifolia*, originally a native of Central America and the Caribbean but now grown around the world, with Madagascar being the primary exporter.

Cultivation

Ideally these orchids need a structure over which to climb. In a commercial setting they are trained over large frames, but indoors they will do well in a basket with a small trellis. A free-draining compost such as peat substitute mixed with sand is recommended, and a regime of moderate watering and feeding should be maintained all year round. Bright natural light is ideal, and in cooler climates the vines will do well in a greenhouse. Most vanilla orchids will not bloom until they have attained a large size.

Vanilla planifolia is widely cultivated for its seed pods, which grow up to 6 inches (15 cm) long. The inflorescences grow along the stem and produce several fleshy sweet-smelling flowers that open one at a time.

Zygopetalum

DATA

Number of Species: About 20.

Classification: *Zygopetalum*
William Hooker 1837; tribe
Maxillarieae, subtribe
Zygopetalinae.

Form: Leaves are long, glossy, and
robust, yellowish to dark green in
color with a prominent midrib
and pointed tip. They sprout
from oval fleshy pseudobulbs.
Long-lived colorful flowers
with long bracts grow on
inflorescences up to 24 in
(60 cm) long.

Distribution: Tropical South
America, mainly Brazil.

Habitat: Humid tropical forests
in lowlands and moderately
hilly country. Some are epiphytes,
growing naturally on the
branches of trees and
shrubs, while others
grow at ground level.

The scientific name *Zygopetalum* translates literally as "yoked petal"
and describes the yoke-shaped structure of the lower flower lip,
which is formed by fused petals and sepals. The flowers are waxy,
intensely scented, and very long lasting, making them popular with
cultivators and florists. The dramatic flowers vary in color and pattern,
with deep reds and purples featuring prominently in many.

Cultivation

Zygopetalum orchids do well indoors. They should be repotted every two
years in specialized orchid compost and fed nitrogen-rich feed monthly
in the first half of the year, with low nitrogen feeds from August onward.
They are intolerant of direct sunlight and high temperatures, so should
not be kept directly under glass. Dark green leaves indicate the plant
needs more light. *Zygopetalum* species cope with warm temperatures by
day as long as they are kept cool at night. Clustering them with other
plants helps maintain humidity. The compost should be kept moist but
not soggy. Do not spray the leaves.

From late fall to early spring *Zygopetalum crinitum* produces three to 10
deeply scented flowers, each measuring just over 3 inches (7.5 cm) across.
This species grows on the ground in the mountains of southern Brazil.

Zygopetalum maculatum

First discovered in southeastern Brazil, *Zygopetalum maculatum* (*Z. mackayi*) is now widely cultivated for its long-lasting flowers. This perennial South American species grows on the ground, in meadows, and in forest glades. There are up to 10 flowers on a single long inflorescence. The striking pale green sepals and petals are decorated with blotches of dark red and the yoke-shaped lip is almost white, with radiating rows of deep pink or purple spots.

Cultivation

Zygopetalum maculatum prefers partial shade. It should be situated in a well-lit spot away from direct sunlight—it will not bloom under florescent light. Water sparingly, but never allow the plant to dry out. It should be grown in a relatively deep pot filled with a freely draining medium such as fir bark. Growth may be encouraged by using a balanced fertilizer in the early part of the year, then switching to a lower nitrogen-high phosphate feed after flowering to help toughen the plant up over the winter.

Classification

Zygopetalum maculatum (Kunth) Garay 1970 (*Zygopetalum mackayi*) William Hooker 1827.

Zygopetalum maculatum

Zygopetalum maxillare

An epiphytic species, *Zygopetalum maxillare* grows naturally on tree ferns at moderate altitudes in the coastal highlands of southeastern Brazil. The leaves are straplike, glossy, and pale yellowish green when receiving the correct amount of light. The waxy flowers bloom in groups of up to eight. The sepals and petals are green with dark red blotches, and the lower lip exhibits a subtle outward gradation from deep pinkish purple to bluish white.

Cultivation

This species should be grown on a block of tree fern. Or, to simulate its naturally restrictive growing situation, use a shallow container filled with a mixture of fir bark and a little sphagnum moss. Disturb the roots as little as possible throughout the life of the plant. Keep the medium moist but not soggy (note that plants growing on a tree-fern slab will be more prone to drying out). Keep out of direct sunlight. On warm days the plant will benefit from a few hours outside, in the light shade of a tree or trellis.

Classification

Zygopetalum maxillare Loddiges 1832.

Zygopetalum maxillare

Zygopetalum Hybrids

Zygopetalum Artur Elle 'Stonehurst'

Zygopetalum Artur Elle 'Derek'

Zygopetalum Blackii 'Negus'

Glossary

Words in SMALL CAPITALS can be looked up elsewhere in the Glossary.

Acicular Needle shaped, usually round in cross section.

Acuminate Having a long sharp point.

Acute Having a short sharp point.

Adventitous (of roots) Arising from an unusual position, such as along a stem rather than from the base.

Aerial Free hanging and exposed to the air.

Aggregate Clustered together.

Anther The terminal part of the male organs (STAMENS) that contain the pollen (*see also* COLUMN, POLLINIUM).

Apex The tip.

Apical Pertaining to the tip or APEX of any part of a plant.

Ascending Growing upward.

Axil The upper angle formed by the union of a leaf with the stem.

Basionym (base name) The first name validly published for a species or genus, which has priority over other names later given to the same species by different authors.

Bi-lobed Having two lobes or earlike projections.

Bract A leaf, often modified or reduced, that subtends a flower or INFLORESCENCE in its AXIL.

Bud blast The withering and dropping of buds from an otherwise healthy plant.

Bulbous Swollen, resembling a bulb.

Caespitose A tufted and clumped growth habit.

Callus A swollen or platelike area on the LIP of an orchid flower.

Calyx All the SEPALS of the flower.

Caudicle The POLLINIUM stalk derived from the ANTHER.

Clavate Club shaped.

Column The central fleshy part of an orchid flower that holds the sexual organs, the STAMEN, and the pistil.

Coriaceous Leathery in texture.

Corm A bulbous underground stem base with scale leaves and adventitious roots, which acts as an organ enabling survival of the plant in harsh times.

Corolla All the PETALS of a flower.

Cristate Crested.

Cylindrical Round in cross section.

Deciduous Shedding leaves in certain seasons, as in orchids that die back to a tuberous root system.

Decurved Curved downward.

Deflexed Bent outward and downward.

Dentate Toothed.

Disk The central upper surface of the LIP, often where the CALLUS occurs.

Distal In a position away from the base and toward the APEX.

Distichous Arranged in two vertical rows.

Dorsal Upper.

Dorsal sepal The uppermost SEPAL in certain orchids.

Elliptical Oval shaped, with narrowed ends.

Endemic Restricted to a particular area or region.

Epichile The tip of the LIP (*see also* HYPOCHILE, MESOCHILE).

Epiphyte An orchid that lives on another plant but does not derive any nutrients from it (*see also* LITHOPHYTE, TERRESTRIAL).

Falciform Sickle shaped.

Fimbriate Fringed with hair or threadlike growths.

Free Not FUSED.

Fused Fully joined to make a complete structure.

Fusiform Spindle shaped.

Galea A helmetlike or hooded structure formed by the DORSAL SEPAL and PETALS of some orchids.

Globular Almost spherical.

Hypochile The basal part of the LIP (*see also* EPICHILE, MESOCHILE).

Imbricate Overlapping like tiles on a roof.

Inflorescence Any arrangement of more than one flower (*see also* RACEME).

Internode The length of stem that lies between two leaf joints (*see also* NODE).

Keel A central DORSAL ridge.

Keiki A plantlet growing directly from either a NODE on the stem of an INFLORESCENCE or from the base of a plant.

Labellum *see* LIP.

Lamina In orchids the broad, flattened middle part of the LIP.

Lanceolate Narrow, as a lance, with tapering ends; widest toward the middle and base (*see also* OBLANCEOLATE).

Lateral Arising from the side.

Leaf axil *see* AXIL.

Ligulate Strap shaped or tongue shaped.

Linear Elongated with parallel sides.

Linear–lanceolate Mid-shaped between LINEAR and LANCEOLATE.

Lip (labellum) The modified, often lobed, third PETAL of an orchid flower.

Lithophyte A plant that grows on stones and rocks and not in the soil (*see also* EPIPHYTE, TERRESTRIAL).

Malesia A region that includes the Malay Peninsula, Indonesia, the Philippines, and New Guinea.

Membranaceous Thin textured and semitransparent.

Mentum A pouchlike or chinlike extension formed by the fusion of the lateral SEPALS and the COLUMN foot.

Mesochile The middle part of the LIP (*see also* EPICHILE, HYPOCHILE).

Monopodial With branches or appendages arising from a simple main axis (*see also* SYMPODIAL).

Montane Relating to or growing in mountain regions, particularly the cool upland slopes.

Mucronate Having a sharp point.

Neem Oil A natural product with antibacterial, antifungal, and antiviral properties; it is also a good source of nutrients. It kills most bugs but is harmless to humans.

Neotropical Relating to the New World (American) tropics.

Node (leaf joint) The point on the stem where one or more leaves or BRACTS are borne.

Oblanceolate LANCEOLATE but tapering toward the base.

Oblong Longer than broad, but blunt at each end.

Obtuse Rounded or blunt.

Ovate Egg shaped.

Pedicel The stalk of a single flower on an INFLORESCENCE.

Pendulous Hanging down.

Perianth All the floral parts of the flower, i.e., the PETALS and SEPALS.

Perlag A coarser form of PERLITE.

Perlite An amorphous volcanic mineral which when added to cultivation media increases aeration, takes up water (but does not become overwet), and does not compact.

Petal One of the sterile parts of the flower that make up the COROLLA, often brightly colored; orchids have three petals which are usually not similar, the two laterals being distinct from the DORSAL, which forms the LIP that is characteristic of orchids (*see also* SEPAL, TEPAL).

Petaloid Petal-like.

Petiolate Having a leaf stalk.

Petiole The stalk of a leaf.

Plicate Folded like a fan.

Pollinium (pl. pollinia) Masses of pollen attached to the COLUMN.

Porrect Directed forward and downward.

ppm (abbreviation) Parts per million.

Proboscis Sucking mouthparts of an insect.

Pseudobulbous Having PSEUDOBULBS.

Pseudobulbs The swollen bulblike stems, often attached to a creeping RHIZOME, of some orchids, from which leaves and flowers may emerge.

Pubescent With soft hairs.

Raceme An INFLORESCENCE consisting of a main axis bearing single stalked flowers; there is no terminal flower so the youngest flowers are nearest the APEX.

Racemose With flowers arranged in a RACEME.

Rachis The main axis (stem) of an INFLORESCENCE.

Raft A wood or tree-fern piece on which to attach an orchid.

Recurved Curved backward and downward.

Reflexed Turned back abruptly.

Rhizome A horizontally creeping underground stem that survives from season to season and from which roots, leaves, flowers, and (in the case of orchids) PSEUDOBULBS emerge.

Rostellum The beaklike outgrowth of the COLUMN that separates the STIGMA from the ANTHER.

Saccate Like a sac or bag.

Saprophyte A plant that cannot live alone but requires decaying organic material as a source of nutrition.

Scape A leafless flower stalk.

Sepal One of the sterile parts of the flower that make up the CALYX, often brightly colored; orchids have three sepals which are usually similar, although the single DORSAL sepal may be elongated (see also PETAL, SYNSEPAL, TEPAL).

Sessile Without a stalk.

Sheath The enclosing base of a leaf or BRACT from which the INFLORESCENCE emerges.

Stamen The male reproductive organ, which in an orchid flower lies at the tip of the COLUMN (see also ANTHER, POLLINIUM).

Staminode A sterile STAMEN.

Stigma The receptive part of the female reproductive organs which in an orchid flower lies on the COLUMN below the ROSTELLUM.

Suberect Upright with a nodding top.

Subsimilar Somewhat similar.

Sulcate Marked with distinct grooves or furrows.

Sympodial A form in which the apparent main stem in fact consists of a series of short axillary branches, each arising from the base of the previous one.

Synsepal A structure formed by the fusion of two or more SEPALS.

Tepal A term describing the three SEPALS and two DORSAL PETALS together when they appear similar.

Terete Cylindrical or tubelike.

Terrestrial Growing in the ground (see also EPIPHYTE, LITHOPHYTE).

Tri-lobed Having three lobes or earlike projections.

Tuber A swollen underground stem or root that lives from season to season.

Tuberoid Resembling a TUBER.

Type The named specimen from which the key characteristics of a species or genus are defined, quite often the first description.

Undulate With wavy sides.

Velamen The protective sheath or coat on some roots.

Further References

REFERENCE BOOKS

Anderson, N., *Letts Guide to Orchids of the World*, New Holland Publishers Ltd., London, 1991.

Bechtel, H., Cribb. P., and E. Laurent, *The Manual of Cultivated Orchids* (3rd edition), The MIT Press, Cambridge, MA, 1992.

Botanica editors, *Botanica's Orchids*, Thunder Bay Press, San Diego, CA, 2002.

Chadwick, A. A., *The Classic Cattleyas*, Timber Press, Portland, OR, 2006.

Christensen, E. A., *Phalaenopsis; A Monograph*, Timber Press, Portland, OR, 2001.

Cullina, W., *Understanding Orchids: An Uncomplicated Guide to Growing the World's Most Exotic Plants*, Houghton Mifflin, Boston, MA, 2004.

Delforge, P., *Orchids of Britain and Europe*, HarperCollins, London, 1994.

Frowine, S. A., *Fragrant Orchids: A Guide to Selecting*, Timber Press, Portland, OR, 2005.

Hawkes, A. D., *Encyclopaedia of Cultivated Orchids*, Faber and Faber, London, 1965.

Keen, P. E., *Wild Orchids across North America*, Timber Press, Portland, OR, 1998.

Kramer, J., *The Conservation International Book of Orchids*, Abbeville Press, New York, 1990.

La Croix, I., *Flora's Orchids*, Timber Press, Portland, OR, 2005.

Lang, D., *Wild Guides: Britain's Orchids*, Wild Guides Ltd., Old Basing, Hampshire, UK, 2004.

Pridgeon, A., *The Illustrated Encyclopedia of Orchids*, Timber Press, Portland, OR, 2006.

Royal Botanic Gardens Kew, *Micropropagation of Orchids at Kew*, Information Sheet K14, 2006.

Siegerist, E. S., *Bulbophyllums and Their Allies: A Grower's Guide*, Timber Press, Portland, OR, 2000.

Stearn, W. T., *Botanical Latin*, Timber Press, Portland, OR, 2004.

Stewart, J., *Orchids of Kenya*, Timber Press, Portland, OR, 1996.

Stewart, J., *Orchids* (revised edition), Timber Press, Portland, OR, 2000.

Stewart, J., and M. Griffiths (eds.), *Manual of Orchids* (New Royal Horticultural Society Dictionary), Timber Press, Portland, OR, 2005.

Stewart, J., and W. T. Stearn, *The Orchid Paintings of Franz Bauer*, The Herbert Press in association with The Natural History Museum, London, 1993.

Tullock, J., *Growing Hardy Orchids*, Timber Press, Portland, OR, 2005.

Watson, J., *Orchid Pests and Diseases* (revised edition), The American Orchid Society, Delray Beach, FL, 2002.

Wood, H. P., *The Dendrobiums*, Timber Press, Portland, OR, 2006.

Zdenek, J., *The Complete Encyclopaedia of Orchids*, Book Sales, London, 2004.

WEB SITES

www.kew.org/wcsp/home.do
A handy checklist giving information on the accepted scientific names and synonyms of monocot plants.

www.mirandaorchids.com
Details of orchids from Brazil.

www.orchidlady.com/pages/encyclopedia/
An online illustrated encyclopedia of orchids.

www.orchids.mu/index.html
Details and photos of numerous orchids.

www.orchids.mu/People/index.html
A useful list of notable botanists and plant hunters, with accepted abbreviations of their names.

www.orchidphotos.org/
A site with photographs of numerous orchids.

www.orchidspecies.com/indexco.htm
A site with details and photographs of numerous orchids.

www.orchidweb.org/aos/
Web site of the American Orchid Society.

www.rhs.org.uk/plants/registerpages/orchidsearch.asp
The International Orchid Register of the Royal Horticultural Society lists officially registered names of orchid hybrids, including details of parentage.

Index

Acknowledgments

Jane Boosey

For my father Bernard George Thompson, with my love and admiration

I wish to thank my co-contributors David Morgan, Amy-Jane Beer, and Dr. Henry Oakeley for their assistance in producing the texts for this book. Special thanks for advice given are also due to: Joyce Stewart (author, orchid taxonomist, and past Director of Horticulture of Royal Horticultural Society Gardens, Wisley); Margaret Ramsey (Micropropagation Unit, Royal Botanic Gardens, Kew); Dr. Henry Oakeley (National Council for the Conservation of Plants and Gardens, National Collection Holder of *Anguloa* and *Lycaste*); and Richard Sanford, Royal Horticultural Society, Wisley.

Picture Credits

t = top, *b* = bottom, *l* = left, *r* = right

Eric Hunt

19, 25, 27, 29, 33, 43, 45, 47, 53, 55, 57, 59, 61, 65, 67, 69, 71, 73, 79, 81, 84, 85*t*, 85*b*, 86, 87, 90–91, 93, 97, 103, 107, 111, 116, 117, 133, 139, 143, 147, 148*t*, 148*b*, 151, 153, 155, 157, 159, 161, 163, 170, 171*r*, 174, 177, 187, 192, 193, 194, 196–7, 198*t*, 198*b*, 199, 209, 211, 217, 219, 223, 224*t*, 224*b*, 225, 227, 233, 235, 241, 244, 246, 247, 248, 249, 251, 253, 257, 259, 261, 263, 265, 267, 271, 273, 275, 279, 293, 294, 295*t*, 295*b*, 299, 303, 315, 317, 319, 320, 321, 322, 323*t*, 323*b*, 325, 327, 331, 333, 339, 341, 351, 353, 355, 371, 373, 376*t*, 376*b*, 377, 387, 389, 391, 397, 399, 400, 403, 407, 414, 415, 419, 421, 423, 431, 437, 439, 441, 443, 445, 447, 453, 455, 459, 465, 471, 473, 477, 483, 491, 493, 499, 501, 503, 507, 509, 511, 513.

Henry Oakeley

39, 41, 283, 285, 301, 305, 307, 309.

Photos Horticultural

1, 2–3, 9, 13, 14*t*, 14*b*, 15, 16, 17, 18, 21, 23, 31, 35, 37, 49, 51, 63, 75, 77, 80, 82–3, 88, 89, 95, 99, 101, 105, 109, 113, 114, 115, 118, 119, 120*t*, 120*b*, 121, 122, 123, 124, 125*t*, 125*b*, 126, 127*t*, 127*b*, 128*t*, 128*b*, 129, 130, 130–1, 131, 135, 137, 141, 145, 149, 165, 167, 169, 171*l*, 172*l*, 172*r*, 173, 175, 179, 181, 183, 185, 189, 191, 195, 200, 201, 203, 205, 207, 213, 215, 221, 229, 231, 237, 239, 243, 245, 255, 269, 277, 281, 287, 289, 291, 297, 311, 313, 329, 332, 334*t*, 334*b*, 335, 337, 342*l*, 342*r*, 343, 344, 345, 347, 349, 357, 358, 359, 360, 361, 362, 362–3, 363, 364, 365, 367, 368–9, 375, 379, 381, 385, 393, 395, 396, 398, 401, 405, 411, 412, 412–3, 413, 416*t*, 416*b*, 417, 427, 429, 432, 433, 435, 449, 451, 457, 461, 463, 467, 469, 475, 479, 485, 487, 489, 495, 497, 504, 505*t*, 505*b*, 514, 514–5, 515.

FLPA
383, 481.

Steve Manning
425.

(*Photos Horticultural wishes to thank: Jane Boosey, Norfolk; Richard Barker, Ipswich; Maureen Halliday, Essex; Bill Gardener, Suffolk; Carol Beddall, Suffolk; Gunilla Hailes, Suffolk; Jeremy Pratt, Suffolk; Wokingham Show Exhibitors, Berkshire; Weston-Super-Mare Show Exhibitors, Somerset; Harrogate Show Exhibitors, Yorkshire; Chelsea Royal Horticultural Show Exhibitors; Michael McIllmurray, National Plant Collection of Maxillaria species; Dave Parkinson Plants at Tatton Show, Cheshire, UK; Roy Barrow, Roydon Orchids; Sara & Brian Rittershausen, Burnham Nurseries Ltd.; Akerne Orchids, Antwerp, Belgium; Essen IMP Show Exhibitors, Germany; Limburg Show Exhibitors, Belgium; Arcen Show Exhibitors, The Netherlands; Orchiflora, Antwerp, Belgium; Orchdeen, Alte Bahn, Germany; Orchideeenhoeve, The Netherlands; Hortus Botanicus, Leiden, The Netherlands.*)